TEN STRATEGIES TO NURTURE OUR SPIRITUAL LIVES

Don't stand still—nurture the life within you

D0861081

LEONARD DOOHAN

REFLECTIONS ON CONTEMPORARY SPIRITUALITY FOR CHRISTIAN ADULTS

ISBN-13: 978-0991006748

ISBN-10: 0991006747

TEN STRATEGIES TO NURTURE OUR SPIRITUAL LIVES
Don't stand still—nurture the life within you

Table of Contents

INTRODUCTION. 1
STRATEGY ONE: APPRECIATE THE CALL TO SPIRITUAL GROWTH. 5
    Identify our experience of faith
    Let our experience of faith be our guide
    Journey in faith to personal and community fulfillment
    Live the challenge of faith in a richer spirituality
STRATEGY TWO: BELIEVE IN THE POWER OF LOVE 13
    Experience God's love
    Journey in love
    Accept the importance of love
    Transform values with love
    Abide in love
STRATEGY THREE: GIVE TIME TO REFLECTION AND PRAYER 23
    Prepare for prayer
    Be calm and have a calming effect on others
    Learn to be receptive
    Think about important things
    Spend time in prayer
STRATEGY FOUR: FIRE UP THE ENERGIES OF OUR SOULS. 33
    Develop our sense of call
    Discern before deciding
    Be single-minded
    Practice patient-urgency
    Enjoy life
    Be generous
    Show compassion
    Live in touch with tradition

STRATEGY FIVE: REMEMBER SUFFERING **45**
  See links between suffering and faith
  Remember suffering
  Respond to suffering
  Answer the call to action
STRATEGY SIX: KEEP HOPE ALIVE **57**
  Live in light of the future
  Be people of hope
  Cultivate hope
  Practice hope
STRATEGY SEVEN: DO GOOD FOR OTHERS **67**
  Focus every day on others
  Bring out the best in others
  Get involved
  Work for peace
STRATEGY EIGHT: OPEN OUR MINDS **77**
  Fight against intolerance
  Welcome new and different ideas
  Support diversity
  Be magnanimous
  Enrich our view of life
STRATEGY NINE: STAY THE COURSE **89**
  Persevere with determination
  Maintain faith
  Accept insecurity and ambiguity
  Risk all
STRATEGY TEN: LIVE YOUR LIFE TO THE FULL **99**
  Strive for a greater share in existence
  Affirm values and vision
  Commit to what is real and true
  Make faith real

"There can be no question in this life of standing still. To neglect a step forward on the path is to take a step backward; to refrain from going up the ladder is to come down; merely to hold one's own in the struggle is to be defeated. Our lives are beset with danger of enemy warfare. Offer no resistance and we perish; resist and we prevail; prevail and victory is ours."

St. Francis of Sales, *Treatise on the Love of God*, Book 3, chapter 1, # 2.

INTRODUCTION

We can't stand still! We must do something. We need to take responsibility for our own personal and communal spiritual growth. When we live motivated by the deepest values of our inner spirit, our lives can be filled with meaning, satisfaction, and fulfillment. It is thrilling for us to bring our spiritual commitment to impact all we are and do, and at times it is difficult for us to explain our enthusiasm to someone who has not crossed this threshold. In this book I offer ten reflections to people like you, men and women who have caught a glimpse of the meaning of life in relation to God. I have met so many of these dedicated individuals who yearn for a deeper personal spirituality and who long to catch a glimpse of values beyond the immediate levels of life. So many relentlessly pursue an understanding of their own destiny, commit themselves to the vision Jesus taught, and seek to be faithful to God's call. If you are one of these, then this book's agenda can help give new focus to your dedication.

This book presents ten challenges that are integral to spiritual growth and help to nurture it. For most of us, and certainly for most readers, faith is rooted in the vision of life presented by Jesus and embodied in the teachings of the Christian community. However, there comes a time when each of us must make this vision our own, and that generally happens as the result of a spiritual experience that shocks us into an awareness that this vision is the only one that gives meaning to our lives. We cannot be passive observers to this vision, but rather we must immerse ourselves in it. We can no longer stand still, we have to do something. Intellectual acknowledgement of teachings that guide our lives is insufficient to lead us to a deeper relationship with God in Christ. Rather, we need a total conversion and transformation of our lives. This often begins with some simple event of daily life that challenges us to rethink the quality of our spiritual growth. Sometimes, experiences of knowing ourselves, or being loved by someone unconditionally, or finding enrichment in community, or knowing and loving another person, all make us think beyond the immediate circumstances, ask why this or that happens, and then we enter a different realm of knowing. At times, we have experiences of the excessive richness of life that make us think of links to life beyond this one; examples could be interpersonal love, childbirth, creativity, forgiveness, and the beauty of the world. Some experiences could stunt our lives but instead lead us to think of transcendent values. Among these would be vulnerability, death, failure, loneliness, and alienation. Then again there are privileged paths in our work or service of others—experiences like war, working for justice, liberating the oppressed, and working with the poor—that cause us to think of more lasting values. All these experiences can become occasions to reassess the depth of our spiritual lives.

Often we cannot reduce these experiences to words; sometimes we just learn, or know, or experience something without being able to explain it. Certain experiences lead to a different kind of knowing. We appreciate Jesus' call in a way we have never grasped before. Whatever the nature of our experience, it becomes reliable, trustworthy, and meaningful to us. It becomes part of our history and self-understanding. We recognize the experience as a gift that transforms our lives. We surrender ourselves to the values of this experience of mystery, which results in an intense spiritual commitment that becomes a way of life for us.

The question that we must now confront is how are we to live out the spiritual values that motivate us—our relationship to Jesus, our fulfillment in community, and our commitment to God, following this experience. This profound personal and transformational experience can come from some simple event of any ordinary day, such as the ones mentioned above, but it gives an understanding of reality and an appreciation of the transcendent, so that our lives are never the same again. We must respond by intensifying our spiritual dedication. It can also arise from the proclamation of the Word of God, or the message of the Christian community, or a religious tradition, but only when it somehow suddenly makes sense to us personally, touches us, calls us, and becomes real for us. This experience of faith may totally permeate our lives. Sometimes it is nothing more than a glimpse of light and illumination in a life of darkness. However, we realize that that experience became a point of departure for a different approach to life for us. We must nourish this spirituality with care and determination. In this book I present ten components of a life that results from faith and nurtures our spirituality. As we become aware of the challenge to live differently, these ten aspects of our spiritual lives enable us to plan carefully to insure that these elements are an integral part of our ongoing commitment.

This book's ten reflections are critical parts of a life of dedication. They are ten strategies for nurturing our spiritual growth. I invite you to think about them, assess their vitality in your own life, share and discuss them with friends, evaluate how individually and with others you can refocus their daily impact, and above all don't stand still but take personal responsibility with others for your spiritual growth.

STRATEGY ONE
APPRECIATE THE CALL TO
SPIRITUAL GROWTH

Identify our experience of faith

In everyone's life there are moments that are very special. These experiences give us insight into the meaning of our lives. They are not only memorable but also transforming, and after such an experience our lives can never be the same again. It seems that we touch something, even someone, beyond the normal horizons of life, and the experience gives us insight beyond all previous knowing. This experience is the basis of faith and a challenge to spiritual growth; it is a call, a personal vocation. We have faith in this new way of looking at reality, we know it is right to do so, and it is this experience that motivates us in all we do.

We can only have faith in something beyond normal horizons of life. In other words, we can only have faith in the transcendent, otherwise we simply have confidence. When Paul says, "I know nothing but Jesus Christ and him crucified" (1 Cor 2:2; see also Gal 2:20), he points to a reality in which he has faith. When John says, "We have come to know that God is love" (1 John 4:16), he expresses faith in a transcendent experience. When a student of mine, having visited the Holocaust museum, told me his life could never be the same again, he had experienced values and insight never before encountered. Although our experience may well be based on some simple event of any day, we feel a sense of wonder and awe that we have caught a glimpse into reality beyond the ordinary. Perhaps in a moment we see we are loved and loveable. Perhaps, we feel anguish at the evil of a world that has lost its values. We may sense that we are redeemed from sin, sinners but forgiven, helpless and empty but filled with transforming love. We may feel someone present to us or ourselves immersed in a presence beyond understanding. We may share in the experience felt by others that Jesus is our savior. We may grasp in a way never done before that the vision of our Church or other religious institutions captures the essence of what it means to give ourselves to God. These daily events that touch transcendent reality fill us with appreciation of a world beyond the present. Our experience could be incremental, appreciating the constant providential care of God for us—small experiences each day until we cannot ignore them anymore. Perhaps, we daily appreciate the wonders and awe of our world, until we hear the call of God in such overwhelming richness.

This experience beyond the normal horizons of life is very personal, and no one else can have this experience for us. In fact, we cannot even control it ourselves. It happens to us. We can only recognize it as a gift of God and receive it with gratitude. We cannot earn this experience, but we can prepare ourselves for it through reflection, peaceful attitudes, and openness to life's richness and beauty. We can also train ourselves to become people of stillness, inspiration, concentration, and silence and thus ready ourselves for insight beyond the normal. Then, we may receive an experience of transcendent life that becomes the source of our faith or vitally confirms belief systems of our past. We appreciate above all that we must now facilitate the growth of this new life.

The experience that calls us to deepen our spiritual commitment is always an experience of God's love or an experience of a world without love; in either case it touches us to the core of our being. It is indescribable, and if we try to explain it to someone else we always feel our descriptions are far less than the reality. The experience is never the same to others as it is to us. In this experience we place our faith, and as a result we live in this world in a new way.

Let our experience of faith be our guide

When we catch a glimpse into a world beyond normal horizons it leads to a conversion, to a new way of knowing and understanding our role in life, and to a new way of knowing and loving God, ourselves, and others. There begins a journey through life when the faith-filled experience becomes our guide. There is something shocking about such a spiritual experience, for it can shatter our previous, neatly packaged knowledge of God and of our role in the world. First, this implies knowing God through what God is not. We find God is not like anything we have previously thought or that others have taught us. That is why spiritual writers and mystics call this journey a way of unknowing, since it implies leaving aside knowledge from our past. At the same time, the transforming experience itself becomes our guide, as we live out the values we learned in our experience. An experience such as this leads to the conviction that we learn more about God and transcendent values in the abandonment of faith than in the accumulated knowledge of the past.

As we focus our spiritual commitment, we grasp before all else a new understanding of ourselves as part of a grander plan that links our lives with others and with a new horizon beyond normal aspects of life. We discover we have a place in the plan of God individually and as a community. Our experience leads us to realize that God loves us; sinners though we may be we experience our redemption; bogged down in a world of confusion and inhumanity we sense hope beyond it all; deprived of love we cry out for its healing presence. This experience gives us a new conception of ourselves, a dignity and destiny, a challenge and a vocation.

We appreciate we have an importance in this life as individuals and as members of a community that we never glimpsed before being drawn to appreciate what lies beyond this life. Living in a new awareness gained from our experience of a touch of grace, we become vitally aware of another realm of life. This is more than an intellectual awareness, for we not only know it but we experience it. We discover this present world does not find meaning in itself but only in the vision of a realm beyond normal horizons of life. A faith-filled spiritual experience opens us to the profound conviction that there is another level of life beyond this one, for we know that we have touched it. Nothing affects the way we live in this life more than the awareness that death is an entrance into a life beyond this one that gives meaning to this one.

We can now live in hope, and can look forward to what we have anticipated. However, we also feel the challenge of what we have experienced, and so living in faith and in hope means daily conversion and transformation. Conversion means a change of heart and a change of outlook on life. We base our personal transformation on the values we saw in our original experience. That experience was of the love, transforming justice, and redemptive purification by God, and we now feel called to journey to a new goal with a new consciousness and gratitude. The experience fills us with gratefulness, wonder, and awareness of God's love, and then we become aware of our own need of personal betterment. Thus, our experience becomes our guide.

Journey in faith to personal and community fulfillment

Living in hope with faith as our guide, we find we must gradually strive to become who we are capable of being and who we are called to become. We find our sense of gratefulness and wonder point to God and call us to personal and community betterment. In other words, we must risk to deepen and nurture our spiritual lives. This journey to fulfillment is first of all a journey of purification of all false concepts of ourselves. At first it creates an inner turmoil as we see so much that is false about ourselves, so much that is inauthentic when placed alongside who we should be. So, in many ways this journey means entering the darkness where at first we are confused and cannot see. Then as our eyes of faith become accustomed to the darkness, we begin to see reality in a new way. Each of us may ask ourselves with new meaning: Where are we? Where are we going? How will we get there? What can we do to help each other to get there? When will we get there?

The journey can be filled with the gift of doubt. Formerly, we may have been so sure of ourselves and our place in the world, but now we question our meaning and purpose in life. Having caught a glimpse of a realm beyond the normal horizons of life, we now feel blessed by doubt about our former convictions. In seeking to clarify our experience, we can move beyond former doubtful certainties to reintegrate our lives with a new focus. We move forward with others and become standards of faith for each other. Our faith gives meaning to what was increasingly meaningless and helps us discover and experience the God who calls us to growth.

If we are truly convinced about the call we felt in our spiritual experience then we will undoubtedly want to move beyond all previous accumulated knowledge that does not give expression to our faith. This will include our former image of God and of ourselves, of the nature of common shared faith, of our relationship to religion, and of the way we ought to live in this life. What at first seems a journey into darkness becomes an experience of illumination. It is not that we cannot see anymore the things we used to see so clearly, but that we find ourselves impelled to see things and to look at things in a different way than we ever did before.

The transforming experience in which we place our faith enthuses us so much that we now peacefully risk all to pursue the life resulting from faith and to courageously persevere with determination. This becomes our asceticism or training for faith-filled living. We discover life's meaning is different than we thought it was. God is not like anything we ever thought of divine life. God treats us differently than we ever imagined. The Church or other religious institutions play a different supportive role than in the past. We have a destiny we never expected. Our relationships with others and with the world are more critically important than ever previously discovered.

Live the challenge of faith in a richer spirituality

If we have encountered God in personal and communal experiences of faith then belief systems and religious traditions can be profoundly helpful in clarifying and maintaining our faith. However, no institution, no system of sanctification, no formal ministry can ever be identified with nor can they substitute for faith. Individuals must pursue faith, nurture it, take responsibility for its growth, and when possible let religion help where it can.

If we cherish our faith, that profound experience of God that transformed our lives, then we will want to live out our faith and in doing so re-experience the great encounter of our lives. As we persevere in faith we will want to frame the issues worth living for and worth dying for. Since the experience of faith is an encounter with the realm of transcendent reality, others will also have similar experiences, and thus we form a faith-filled community. There is a communal dimension to faith, a community that supports and becomes a standard of faith. Many churches do this admirably.

Our persevering commitment to faith means reliving the core values of the experience beyond normal horizons. Sharing with others who have had similar experiences enlarges our appreciation of the implications of faith. Former individuals of faith can also be models who help us to articulate the consequences of faith, and fellow Christians and people from other religious traditions can inspire and motivate us. Above all, faith calls us to live with a new sense of personal vocation and dedication. We are primarily the people who must be accountable for what we experience. We appreciate the call to spiritual growth and the challenge to take all necessary steps to achieve it. We can no longer stand still and do nothing. God gives to each of us special moments of insight into our purpose in life. We must take these moments seriously and never let them pass unanswered.

Key reflections:

- Reflect on which particular values you learned as a result of the most profound, transforming experience of your life.
- Savor for a while an experience when you felt God's love touch you in a special way.
- What role does community play in your experience of faith?
- Think about how your life has changed because of your faith experience.

Action items:

➢ Identify at what point in your life you began to live in a different, value-centered way, and decide why.
➢ Specify what you think your role is in the plan of God.
➢ Describe three or four core convictions that motivate you in daily life.

➢ If you are a member of a church or other religious organization give three advantages of belonging and three disadvantages of such a relationship.

Focus questions for one's journal:

Identify your experience of faith.

Have you ever felt a special call? Describe it.

Explain the circumstances when you experienced something beyond the normal events of life.

How do you train yourself to appreciate the wonderful moments of life?

Describe an occasion when you felt loved in a profound way.

Let your experience of faith be your guided

How do you understand the concept of God?

Describe how your faith has led you to think of yourself in a different way.

What gives meaning to your present life?

Describe how your faith guides you on a daily basis.

Journey in faith to personal fulfillment

Address the four key questions of your life: Where am I? Where am I going? How will I get there? When will I get there?

Describe something that you were formerly convinced of that you now question.

Do you find yourself looking at things in a different way than you used to? Give an example.

Explain simply the meaning of your life now, and compare it to what you thought five years ago.

Live the challenge of faith in a richer spirituality

What for you is worth living for and worth dying for?

Who is a model for you in faith?

What are the key values of your faith? List four or five.

Planning for Strategy One: Clarify the nature of faith.

1. List three important goals you see as part of your call to faith.

2. What are your personal gifts that could help you attain these goals?

3. Specify any weaknesses that could stunt your growth in faith.

4. Who are the significant others who journey with you?

5. How will you achieve these resolutions?

6. When will you do this?

7. Will you do this alone or with others? With whom?

8. How will you evaluate how successful you have been?

Topics for group discussion or sharing.
1. What does faith mean to you, individually and as a group?
2. How is your daily life different because of your faith?
3. Describe how you see the relationship between faith, beliefs, and religion.
4. What is the vocation of this group?

STRATEGY TWO
BELIEVE IN THE POWER OF
LOVE

Experience God's love

Increasing numbers of men and women feel called to live motivated by a faith-filled experience that impacts, convinces, and transforms their lives. We, too, can courageously pursue this journey to God which is also a journey to an appreciation of our own uniqueness and destiny in life. Our spiritual conviction is always in God's love of us, and the resulting journey we want to undertake is a journey to a deeper understanding of the centrality of love in our lives. After all, a faith-filled spiritual experience is essentially an encounter with God who is a loving community, and who blesses us and calls us to stand firm in love, to live motivated by that love, to abide in that love, and to respond with love (see Ephes 1:13-14). Faith convinces us that we are new creatures, born anew because God has planted within us a seed of the divine life of love that now grows on its own. Faith means appreciating that we are an integral part of God's strategy of love. God is love, lives in a loving community, creates the world to extend love, becomes incarnate as proof of love, lives in love, teaches love, and commands us all to live in love as proof of our faith (John 13:34-35).

Experiencing God's love is a learning situation for us. We learn the importance of love in our spiritual lives, see the example of love in God's approach to this world and to ourselves, and know the gift includes a challenge to live this love in spiritual depth. In thinking about God, scrutinizing and seeking answers to questions of belief and religion are not enough; we must transform ourselves by love. Unfortunately, contemporary life has so many examples of people who proclaim their belief, establish agendas based on their belief systems and religion, argue their positions forcefully, and defend their views violently. But God is not known by what we think or by our arguments, no matter how persuasive we may think they are. Rather, we experience God in love, and we know God through lives based on love.

We seek meaningful lives based on the initial God-given experience of love. It is a far different awareness to find that "The Father himself loves you" (John 13:34-35) than to listen to doctrine and discipline. Our experience forces us to take a stand and to live differently because we know we are loved. Our own awareness enables us to glimpse transcendent reality—that it is love that is the basis for life in this world and for life beyond the normal realms of experience.

Journey in love

The spiritual journey of men and women does not begin with our effort-filled attempts to discover God. Rather, the journey begins with God who in love for us draws us towards divine life. Our responsibility is to let go of false and selfish values that tie us down. Cutting the cords of false values enables God to then draw us to divine life. So, the point of departure is God's love of us not our love of God. The journey is less one of faith and more one of love, or we may say it is a journey of faith in love. As faith purifies our ways of knowing God, so the journey of love purifies our ways of loving God. It is a journey in which we deepen our awareness of God's transforming love of us and in which we also deepen our love of God and of others.

Thus, our entire spirituality becomes one of persevering together in love. Jesus never suggested that the world around us would be transformed by faith, but he did say, "Everyone will know that you are my disciples, if you have love for one another" (John 13:35; see also John 17:23). Journeying through life in love must touch every aspect of life and integrate them all in total dedication to

God, loving "the Lord your God with all your heart, and with all your soul, and with all your mind" (Matt 22:37).

As we respond to our experience of God's love we journey onward, daily making decisions based on love. This is not merely the accumulation of small manifestations of love but more particularly decisions of choice for what is always the best and most loving thing to do. At times these decisions make us who we are; they are creative of our personalities. These decisions imply sacrificing something that is good, but at the same time they open us to creative dimensions of quality love.

This journey of love is the most faithful way to be a Christian in our contemporary world. We must rediscover the centrality of community. Ours is a world that cries out for healing and redemptive love. Jesus hoped we would be models of love, but often Christians are not. We argue, our communities become polarized, we fight each other, and few people know that our profession is to share with others the love we have received. If we Christians could recommit ourselves to the greatest commandment, we could transform our world.

The most important dimension of our journey to love is to become immersed in God's love for us. Just as there is a dark night of faith, so too there is a dark night of love. We find God does not act towards us as we thought God would. When we thought God would be close to us in our need, God withdraws and seems to leave us alone, feeling rejected. Even when in union with God in loving prayer, we get the distinct impression of a distance between us. Through these partial presences, withdrawals, and absences, we learn to abandon false ways of loving and to journey with single-mindedness and single-heartedness to an authentic vision.

Accept the importance of love

Love is important to us primarily because our belief and faith enlighten us to the realization that God is love. The inner life of the Trinity shows that the relationship of love is of the divine essence. Since we are made in God's image and likeness, we are made to live in love, both divine and human. Moreover, the whole of salvation history as described in Scripture details God's strategy of love for humanity—every generation is part of this ongoing plan. Scripture describes God's loving care, guidance, redemptive correction, and ongoing challenge of humanity to live in love. Jesus, the beloved of the Father, comes filled with enduring love, calling everyone to share in that love. His major teachings all focus on love, and his new commandment is that humanity respond in love. Many unusual episodes in Jesus' ministry—disclosure situations—focus on the fact that love is more important to him than all else. These aspects of biblical spirituality demand that we take a stand in life to always give priority to what is the most loving thing to do.

Love is also important because we are born into this world of God's love. Like fish in water, this world of God's love is the atmosphere in which our own human nature can flourish. The creation and our own beginnings are because of God's love, and our end is to live in God's love in a realm beyond the normal horizons of this life. Furthermore, love is also the means to move from one to the other. In other words, we dedicate ourselves to a spirituality based on Christian love. The history of spirituality evidences many paths to self-purification, growth, and identification with God, but the path of love is the short cut to transformation, even though it is also the straight, narrow, and steep road to spiritual growth.

The conviction on the importance of love in Christian growth is highlighted in over two millennia of Christian writers and mystics. So many of them when choosing a central issue to describe the Christian's journey to God stress love. Writers and theologians in their reflection and study draw this conclusion, as do mystics in their recounting of their experiences. Thus, we have sermons on love, commentaries on the love poem of the *Song of Songs*, theological discourses on the stages of love of God. Then we have many extraordinary works of mystics, like the poem on love by Hadewijch of Antwerp, "The Fire of Love" by Richard Rolle, "Revelations on Divine Love" by Juliana of Norwich, "The Living Flame of Love" by John of the Cross, and "Treatise on the Love of God" by Francis of Sales.

It is also important to refocus on love as a corrective to some of the non-evangelical agendas of some contemporary Churches. Religions always build hedges of rules and regulations around their central convictions. The universal problem with this practice is that the emphasis on secondary rules distracts from the primary core values, and this emphasis becomes an obstacle to living central values. This has happened to Christian love, and unfortunately only a few Christian groups and leaders are known as prophets of love. We need to change the direction of our lives and reclaim the central importance of love.

Transform values with love

We cannot merely believe in the power of love, we must act on that conviction and show our dedication in action. This means making decisions based on the most loving thing to do. When we live in this way, we ourselves are the first focus of transformation. We change our own attitudes to life, rejecting selfishness, greed, and self-satisfaction, and thus we move away from self-centeredness to self-transcendence. This is a rigorous self-training and eventually leads to the integration of all aspects of life in loving self-gift to God. This single-hearted pursuit of the way of love transforms our decisions, actions, and purposes in life.

When we are motivated by our conviction of the transforming value of love, we treat others with a natural benevolence. We wish them well before any encounter, appreciate the good in others, and presume that they will do good. This positive, optimistic approach to others has a healing effect on relationships and opens up the development of friendships that are mutually enriching. The development of love-based friendships prepares us for our journey of love and the fostering of deeper relationships with other people in community and with God.

People who believe in the power of love can approach the development of their own family life in a new enriched way. Family provides the basic encounter of love and is ideally also a school of love where all members can learn from each other and reach out beyond the boundaries of family life to spread their treasure of love to others. The family group is a community of love wherein human qualities mature. Husband, wife, and children, in total solidarity, enrich one another and together bring into being human values otherwise unattainable. Family life, seen as a domestic Church, is also the foundation of Church life, and when love is strong in the former it helps build up the latter. In fact, the Church is a family of families, and the Church described the family as "a covenant of love" (Church Today 47:2).

There is an intimate connection between our individual growth in love and our growth as communities of love. Unfortunately, we do not always see loving communities, and the contemporary challenge for those who believe in the power of love is to foster reconciliation. St. Paul summed up the whole thrust of Jesus' ministry as the work of reconciliation and saw his own ministry as one of reconciliation (2 Cor 5:18-19). As Christians, working for reconciliation is an essential dimension of our call in faith to love others. This includes repentance, a change of mentality, and mutual forgiveness. It also means reaching out to the marginalized or rejected, respecting others' opinions, and building bridges. Bringing others together in reconciliation strengthens our common dedication to pursue the way of love. When we understand the transforming power of love, it becomes the source of our energy to change unacceptable realities

Abide in love

Generally, a faith-filled experience is an experience of abiding in God's love. It may last only a short time, but it produces an understanding of the real values of life. It is an intimacy which changes all future relating to God and to others because of our new relationship with God. This new approach to God is based on Jesus' own relationship to his Father. "As the Father has loved me, so I have loved you; abide in my love" (John 15:9). It becomes an ever deepening relationship between us as disciples and Jesus. "Abide in me as I abide in you" (John 15:4). Believing in the power of love, we become ever more aware that we must make every effort possible to maintain this relationship, knowing that like branches we draw life from union with the vine.

Abiding in God's love is not passive but implies a dynamic ongoing fidelity to the vision of faith. It is an awareness of the presence and power of the Spirit of God within us. It means being faithful to Jesus' teachings (John 14:23; see also 1 John 3:23-24), especially the greatest commandment to love one another (John 13:34). Our daily dedication to faithfully live Jesus' teachings and to love one another shows we cherish our faith and we believe in the power of love. At a time when there is so much hatred in our world, we Christians can take a prophetical stance and proclaim by words and deeds the value of living together in faith-filled love.

We discover there is a mutual interrelationship between learning from our experience of God's love for us and how that impacts our relating to God. Our affectivity should not be divided between several objects but integrated into one total self-commitment in love that changes every aspect of our relating both to this world and to a world beyond this one. So we can learn from our experience of God's love how we ought to love others unconditionally, respecting them, forgiving their failures, finding their best gifts, sharing with them as God has done for us. Then we can learn in interaction with others what they hope for, how they seek meaning in life, why they value mutuality and bring all these learning moments into our own relating to God.

Abiding in Jesus' love means dedicating ourselves to the service of others in society. Jesus came to bring us the Father's love and insisted he came to serve others and thus give an example of the implications of love. He washed the disciples' feet during the Last Supper as a symbolic action of the consequences of love. So, abiding in love leads to a leavening effects on the whole of society and thus manifests the power of love.

Key reflections:

- How do you experience the power of God's love in your life?
- Think about ways in which you are self-centered and ways in which you move away from self to focus on others
- Reflect on what are the false, unloving values of your life.
- Name the priorities of local churches or other religious organizations, and then name your own.

Action items:

- ➢ In the next few days deliberately make decisions based on the most loving thing to do.
- ➢ Pick two areas where you know you must practice reconciliation to someone else and plan accordingly.
- ➢ Identify and commit yourself to several areas of service of others in your daily working life.

> Discuss with your spouse and family how together you can be a school of love for others, and how this love can provide the incentive for personal growth.

Focus questions for one's journal.

Experience God's love

> What does faith teach you about God's love?
>
> Give examples of God's love for you.
>
> Do you live differently because of your faith?

Journey in love

> How have your ways of showing love for God changed in recent years?
>
> Do people recognize you as a disciple of Jesus because of your love?
>
> How are your decisions based on love?
>
> What sort of an impact on the world do you have as a Christian?
>
> Describe an occasion when you expected to experience God's love but felt you didn't.

Accept the importance of love

> Why do you think God loves you?
>
> How does love motivate your life?
>
> Name a book on love that inspired you.
>
> Does your church center all its teachings on love?

Transform values with love

> Do your decisions evidence a priority for love?
>
> How do you treat other people?
>
> Is your family or group of friends a school of love for others?
>
> With whom are you not reconciled and why?

Abide in love

> How do you abide in the love of the Lord?
>
> Would Jesus be proud of you as someone who loves others in his name?
>
> Is the power of your love spread out over many objects or integrated?
>
> How do you show an attitude of service for others?

Planning for Strategy Two: Believing in the power of love.

1. List three important goals of your call to believe in the power of love.

2. What are your gifts that could help you attain these goals?

3. Specify any weaknesses that could stunt your growth in this call to believe in the power of love.

4. What can you do in the short term to achieve these goals?

5. How will you achieve these resolutions?

6. When will you do this?

7. Will you do this alone or with others? With whom?

8. How will you evaluate how successful you have been?

Topics for group discussion or sharing.

1. Share with the group a profound experience of God's love for you.
2. Why do each of you think you are loveable?
3. Give examples of decisions each of you has made that exemplify you were basing your decisions on what was the most loving thing to do.
4. What do you think you as a group can teach others about love?

STRATEGY THREE
GIVE TIME TO REFLECTION
AND PRAYER

Prepare for prayer

Each time I go to London, I like to see Westminster Abbey, and on the archway that leads to the canons' quarters, there is a little brass plaque that reads, "There are four acts of prayer; stillness of body, inspiration by the Spirit, concentration with Christ, and silence in God." While these may well be four components of prayer, they are also, and more importantly, four preparatory tasks to reflection. If we train ourselves to reflect, prayer will come naturally. The latter is a gift, the former is our responsibility.

In times past, spiritual writers and guides spoke about the prayer of the body, by which they meant the efforts we make to ready our bodies for reflection and prayer. These efforts include good posture, stillness, breathing correctly, and healthy diet. No one can reflect meaningfully when he or she is distracted, compulsive, hurried, breathing erratically, or suffering the consequences of overeating or overdrinking. So, the first task is to be still, relaxed, with our bodies trained to contribute to the mind's and heart's reflection.

A second task that prepares us for reflection is training ourselves in inspiration. This means giving time to whatever we do, being completely present to people and events, so we can see the inner values and goodness around us. A person prepared to reflect is one who can be inspired by the beauty of nature, by a wonderful piece of music, by artistic brilliance, by children's simplicity, by others' love, goodness, and dedication. Inspiration means we can discover the inner spirit of events and people. If we can, then we are ready to be inspired by the transcendent in moments of reflection. If we can be inspired by the wonders found in the ordinary, then we will be ready to be inspired by the Spirit.

The third preparatory task to reflection is to learn to concentrate. Quick decisions, sound bites, one minute podcast summaries, multitasking, texting, and so on, all have value, but all diminish our ability to concentrate. We live with overviews and superficiality now more than ever. Concentration is an essential component of reflection and prayer. We can train ourselves to concentrate on conversation, on a passage of Scripture, on a piece of music, on a glass of good wine, on a poem, on a child's schoolday events, on a friendship. Concentration helps us see things we otherwise would not, to value people in ways we never imagined, to see the heart of issues that we never used to, and to concentrate with Christ on the great issues of life.

The fourth preparatory task to reflection is the ability to remain in silence. In a world filled so often with noise and distractions, we rarely have opportunity to be quiet, empty, and receptive. We are so full of secondary issues that we cannot get our fill of the values of God. We are blocked by immediate clutter that prevents us from perceiving realities beyond the normal horizons of life. We need to train ourselves to gain distance from the noise, be alone, let nothing happen, sense our emptiness and need, and listen for voices and insights we can never hear without silence. We must train ourselves to cultivate a spirit of watchful waiting for God's interventions in our lives and to silently rest in God.

Be calm and have a calming effect on others

A quality that fosters, maintains, and strengthens our spiritual life is calmness. If we work to become people of inner peace and tranquility we will focus on essentials, prioritize major issues of life with grace, and treat others with respect and graciousness. To maintain calmness we need to be comfortable with ourselves, never afraid to be alone, and to be peaceful in dealing with the anxious challenges our lives bring. Much anxiety is caused by false attachments in life—we become attached to things we do not need, to our own opinions that are no better than others', to dominant roles we do not need, and to dreams that would not help us even if we attained them. We must let go and let be, or in the ideas of spiritual writers become detached from these false and distracting desires. Rather, we can be at ease with our own strengths and weaknesses, calmly appreciative that authenticity is found in our hearts; not by having more or doing more, but by being more.

In fostering a sense of calmness in life, we need to eliminate certain negative attitudes that distract us in our lives. We must check any kind of compulsive behavior that thwarts our inner peace. We should control any spirit of complaining that can infect our lives and detrimentally affect others. We need to change constant negativity into a positive, optimistic, and enthusiastic approach to life and to others. Furthermore, we must avoid overdoing things and learn to say "no" to more distractions and "yes" to quality time and presence for others and for God.

Good choices preserve and strengthen calmness and inner peace. So, let us choose the company of people who appreciate quality of life and avoid overly competitive people many of whom seem always angry and disturb our peace. Let us choose daily exercise to have its healing effects on our lives. We can always do something different than we usually do to alleviate boredom. Let us choose friends who strengthen our approach to life, and let us appreciate them as gifts.

One of the ways to train ourselves to be calm, and thereby have a calming effect on others, is to develop a correct approach to leisure. Leisure requires free time and relaxation, and can lead to creative self-development. But, it is also an attitude to life that renews and re-energizes our inner selves. In other words, leisure can enrich our personal inner spirit, prepare us for reflection on the deepest of human, spiritual values, and open our hearts to think about, express, and experience faith. It is in times of leisure that we can open our minds and hearts to think beyond the ordinary and ready ourselves for self-transcendence and transformation.

Maintaining our own inner calm helps us have a calming effect on others. They can discern we are people of reflection and feel challenged to become more reflective themselves. Calmness fosters new friendships of like-minded people. It opens our minds to new opportunities. Our own inner calm helps diminish stress and fosters healthy living. Furthermore, our own calmness leads to quality presence and encourages others to be enriched in similar ways.

Learn to be receptive

Training ourselves to be reflective and prayerful allows us to appreciate our faith. But, faith is a gift; we do not earn it. Rather, when we are empty, we can receive it gratefully. This means our emphasis is not on doing or achieving but rather on being passive and receptive. We need to be skillful in finding opportunities to reflect on what is happening around us and within our own minds and hearts. To do this we can train ourselves to sit still and do nothing, to listen intensely to sounds around us and to what people say or do not say, to look at things until we see the extraordinary beyond the ordinary, to refine all our senses so that we receive more intensely what happens around us. Being receptive leads to breakthrough perceptions more than accumulated activities do.

One of life's gifts that we appreciate more through reflection is time. The ancient world offered three approaches to time. "Tempus" was historical time, "chronos" was measured time that consumes our lives with its many demands, and "kairos" was a time of grace and blessing. We can foster the third approach to time which is grace, opportunity, free-flowing, and a new pace of living. We can rejoice and appreciate the gift that time can be for us—time to reflect, to be who we want to be, and to receive its many gifts. This is quiet open-ended time in which faith becomes real again; it is our own sacred time.

For reflective people, the world is also their guru; it is a sacred place which teaches us so much about life. People of spiritual depth appreciate the material world with its natural beauty, with its wonders that call forth worship of the creator, and with its cycles of nature that can enlighten us about life. What the world does naturally we can create in our own special places which facilitate reflection and prayer. Some places we find beautiful, some music we find uplifting, and together they aid in creating an environment conducive to reflection. In a busy world we need to be skillful in setting aside special spaces that aid us in thinking about the essential values of this life and the next.

We learn to be open, receptive, and appreciative of time and place, but also of people whose goodness, beauty, dedication, and love can inspire us, bring us calm in a hectic world, encourage us to peace in troubled times, and call us to be the best people we are capable of being. Reflecting on other people's dedication, passion, and enthusiasm can call forth the same qualities in us. As reflective people, we never forget how other people are gifts to us.

Think about important things

As people moved by spiritual values, we must spend our time on important issues. Our world is immersed in superficiality, but the experience of faith teaches us that this life is part of a life beyond present, visible horizons. There are times for joy, pleasure, satisfaction, and shared celebration—all appropriate manifestations of our daily life. However, contemplative people realize that ours is a world in need of transformation, and we must think about this creatively and work to attain it. Our spirituality challenges us to strive for the love in which we believe.

Early Christians gave much of their reflection time to the memory of the passion and death of Jesus. This reminded them, as it does us, of the horrors of suffering, of the evils of deliberately inflicting suffering on others, of the fact that our sinful attitudes cause the suffering, and that the patient endurance of suffering to save others is a great sign of transforming love. People throughout our world, some of whom represent us, have refined the inflicting of suffering on others, justify it for pseudo-political reasons, and become hard-hearted in the process. We must always think about suffering in our world, try to understand it from the perspective of those who suffer, and dedicate ourselves to alleviate suffering wherever we find it

Unless our commitment is merely lip service to intellectual statements of belief, we will always struggle with issues of social justice. Our world in general, our political, business, healthcare, and religious institutions are in a mess, and we have to focus on matters of social justice, since few in authority ever do. Oppression of the poor, neglect of the sick, abuse of workers and investors, sexual perversion, genocide, the aggression of wars, are all daily events in the so-called civilized world. This has been the case for over two thousand years, and we still fail, but our commitment to spiritual growth must challenge us to reform these failures. When will it end unless people of faith, dedicated to love, keep these atrocities always before our minds and hearts, and work for reform and the correcting of society's values.

Part of all efforts to work for social justice will be a commitment to ethics. Many people were largely absent from challenging the crimes of war, the destruction of many lives in the greed of business, the deliberate unwillingness to transform healthcare, the systematic abuse of women and children, the prostitution of political and governmental institutions, and the rape of the environment. We need to individually think about these important issues and work for a reform of ethics to the broader issues of life.

Reflective people will also think about the important issue of leadership. Today, many leaders are arrogant autocrats, failed facilitators, blind visionaries, narcissists, deaf prophets, ignorant and incompetent officials. Many people have given up on their leaders and no longer expect them to do anything worthwhile. This is equally true in politics, business, healthcare, and religion. If we were really able to choose our leaders we would choose few, if any, of those who hold office today. As we reflect on the problems created by our leaders we can determine to accept and support only those who stand for the essential values of our faith. No leader has a right to our respect and allegiance; each one must earn it. In times of reflection, we must think about these and other important issues.

Spend time in prayer

With spiritual sensitivity, we think things through, reflect, and constantly examine our lives—all part of an attitude of discernment regarding life's values and directions. As people who have had a faith-filled experience that revealed connections between the here and now and a realm of life beyond the ordinary dimensions of our world, we seek to maintain that link through prayer. Vocal and community prayer can help. But they are too wordy and too full of us to be significant other than as remote forms of prayerful reflection.

Prayer is a relationship of love between a person and God. We bridge the span between our life and loving union with God in life beyond this one through various forms of communication. At first, we tend to fill these times of communication with many words, thoughts, hopes, requests, and promises. However, we need to think less and talk less in prayer and just learn how to be quietly present to God. Friends do not need to talk all the time, neither do lovers, nor do people of faith and shared spiritual values. Rather, as time passes, words are less important, and people just like to spend time together.

Being present to God in prayer gradually means letting go of former ways of knowing and loving God and opening our hearts to new experiences. This is a time of simplification of prayer and of the laying aside of prayer structures and methods that we once controlled so well. Prayer gradually consists of few words, few thoughts; it is more a loving attention to God. Put briefly, this stage means talking less and loving more.

As we give ourselves to God in prayer, it seems normal to expect that the loving relationship will intensify and unfortunately it does not. In the long run it will return in a different form, but not for some time. Dedicated to prayer, we must first enter the darkness that brings disorientation, sadness, pain, insecurity, and even a sense of abandonment. Rather than intensify the relationship of love in prayer, God often withdraws, acts differently than we ever expected, withholds love, and leaves us alone. This is a period of darkness that purifies a human being's way of relating to God. It is a painful experience but one we will look back on with joy and peace.

Our final way of relating to God in prayer is to be open to receive. We have learnt that our contribution amounts to removing obstacles of a false self, an inaccurate understanding of prayer, and a too-human perception of God. Our primary response is openness and receptivity, letting God transform us in every aspect of our being. The strategy of giving time to reflection and prayer is a decision for depth, enrichment, and transformation in our spiritual lives. Being constantly connected to God through prayer helps empty us of selfishness and brings us the power to be our true selves.

Key reflections:

- Think about how you can become a person of calmness, inner peace, and tranquility.
- Consider how you can become more reflective and more receptive.
- How do you view and use time?
- Examine your own life to see if you spend more time on important issues or on trivial ones.

Action items:

➤ Practice a little stillness, inspiration, concentration, and silence.
➤ Strategize to eliminate obstacles to inner peace.
➤ Make sure you have healthy leisure periods in every day.
➤ Spend a little time in reflection and prayer every day, reducing words and thoughts and simply being present to God.

Focus questions for one's personal journal.

Prepare for prayer
How do you prepare for prayer?
Describe how you prepare your body for prayer.
What inspires you?
Give examples of when you concentrate during the day.
What are your silent times?
Be calm and have a calming effect on others
Are you comfortable with yourself?
Are you compulsive about anything?
Who among your friends disturbs your inner peace?
What are your attitudes to leisure?
Do people like your company? Why do you think they do?
Learn to be receptive
Describe an episode when you were receptive and fulfilled.
Think about your use of time—is it tempus, chronos, or kairos?
What do you learn from the world around you?
Who is a special gift to you at this time and why?
Think about important things
Are you a contemplative person?
Do you often think about important issues?

When do you give thought to the serious issues of our world?
Do you think your church is a voice against injustice?
What do you think about today's leaders in politics and the Church?

Spend time in prayer

Do you pray regularly?
Describe what your prayer is like.
How can you simplify your prayer?
Describe an experience of darkness in your prayer.
How do you give God a chance to transform you?

Planning for Strategy Three: Giving time to reflection and prayer.

1. List three important goals that would help you improve your prayer.

2. What are your personal gifts that could help you attain these goals?

3. Specify any weaknesses that could stunt you giving time to reflection and prayer.

4. What can you do in the short term to achieve these goals?

5. How will you achieve these resolutions?

6. When will you do this?

7. Will you do this alone or with others? With whom?

8. How will you evaluate how successful you have been?

Topics for group discussion or sharing.

1. How does your daily life prepare each of you for prayer?
2. What disturbs your calmness and thus hinders your prayer?
3. Share with each other how you think you have learned to be receptive.
4. Let each one describe how his or her prayer has changed in recent years.

STRATEGY FOUR
FIRE UP THE ENERGIES OF
OUR SOULS

As people dedicated to spiritual growth we need to know our own inner strengths and energies and use them effectively to maintain our own value systems and to positively impact our surrounding environment. Some of us will have different strengths than others, and we can complement each other in our communities of faith. But there are some common forces for good that can energize us all. Below I present some key energies that are important to me and I hope also to you.

Develop a sense of call

Each of us needs to rediscover our call in life and faithfully pursue it with fortitude. The core values that motivate our lives give rise to an awareness of our enduring purpose in life. In other words we see things that we can do well and that seem to consistently do good to others. The good that we consistently do because of the gifts we have becomes part of our mission in life.

We can deepen this awareness of what we can do well for the common good and make it a firmly established part of our lives. We feel called to respond in ways we know affect others and our environment positively. This sense of call points us to our own destiny in life. It cannot be sporadic or episodic, but it needs to be a deliberate part of our self-concept. Knowing we have a calling energizes us and intensifies the good we can do. We arrive at a point where we cannot ignore this drive for goodness within ourselves; rather we are unable to do anything but intensify it. It is a vocation, and the personal integrity of each of us relates to us faithfully following this call.

Feeling we are in this world for a reason is a spiritual awakening, and once we identify it then this sense of call develops an internal dynamic of its own. It grows within us, clarifying this important aspect of our personalities. Faithfully following our call is an inward journey of self-discovery, a life-changing journey during which we find our role in the plan of God. Few aspects of life energize us more than knowing we can never be our true selves without faithfully pursuing this call.

When we become aware of our own calling, we also see ourselves within a larger context. Call in this world has no meaning outside an awareness of another realm of life. Thus, a sense of call relates directly to our spiritual growth. When we confront ourselves in the larger context of the meaning of life, we see ourselves more clearly than at any other time. We cannot make excuses or decide we do not wish to respond. In the experience we see ourselves immediately in relationship to God and see ourselves exactly as we are, with our strengths and our gifts, and immediately know that we have a calling that we must pursue.

Discern before deciding

Life is complicated, and we are constantly faced with making decisions that reflect the values of our faith-filled experiences and spiritual commitment. At every turn in life we must choose freely between various alternatives. Nowadays, there are no easy answers; situations change rapidly, authorities do not have pre-packaged answers like they used to, and the "right" response is not always evident. We make choices with humility, knowing we will often be wrong. However, with humility and courage we must choose, for to refuse to make a decision that reflects our values is itself a decision with serious implications.

Discernment is an inner energy by which we assess alternatives in light of our spiritual commitments. It is a self-training to make judgments based on values that we want to guide our lives. It is not haphazard but a specific method of reflecting, assessing alternatives, clarifying implications of decisions, and opening our hearts to the guidance of the Holy Spirit. At first it takes significant time, but with practice we can do it very speedily, almost intuitively. This critical analysis of alternatives is a judgment made in light of our vision of life. It is an exercise of wisdom. Too many people do not think enough before making decisions and so do not deliberately impact their environment with their values.

Discernment requires honesty, openness, and prayerfulness. It also calls for flexibility, foresight, and creativity. It means being a good listener—to self, others, the world, the signs of the times, the hopes of humanity, and the cries of the needy and suffering. Judgments need to be based on what we discern to be the best thing to do in any given situation, and to do that effectively we must be open to the signs of goodness, justice, and love, and sensitive to cries against evil, injustice, and hatred. Then, in light of our values we can choose which alternative is best and make judgments accordingly.

Discernment is an energy of the spirit. When practiced consistently it helps us live intentionally and deliberately in light of the values of our faith-filled experiences. It can gradually transform our lives, focusing them in ways that help us become who we want to be and to be known for the values for which we want to be known.

Be single-minded

A particularly significant energy of the spirit that furthers commitment to a depth of spiritual dedication is single-mindedness. This attitude is mentioned in the Bible as a beatitude: "Blessed are the pure in heart, for they will see God" (Matt 5:8). So, we are talking about an uncontaminated pursuit of the values that guide our lives. In the Bible, heart is as much the source of knowledge and conviction as it is of love. Single-mindedness or single-heartedness focuses on implementing values. It is the relentless pursuit of integrity, making sure our lives always reflect the values of our inner spirit.

Single-mindedness refers to clarity of purpose in life, a daily determination to be faithful to values that motivate us. We always need to complement this energy of the spirit with humility. Because we are determined about something does not mean we are always right. After all, there are many world leaders, national leaders, and maybe even friends of ours who confuse stubbornness and arrogance with the single-minded pursuit of values. Rather, we need to pursue our values with humility, listening to the challenges of others, purifying when necessary. Change and effort to refocus preserve the uniqueness of the values we pursue.

We live in a complex world where people have different value systems. Some values we will hold in common, but others no. Our single-minded pursuit of motivating values is always within the context of other good people's pursuit of their value systems. So, single-mindedness is lived out with courageous determination and also with mutual respect for innumerable differences resulting from history, culture, religious traditions, and so on.

For each of us, single-mindedness is an energy of the spirit that manifests the depth of awareness of our call and of the conviction that comes through discernment. It shows forth our integrity, the balance between what we experience and how we live following that experience. The Bible says such people "will see God": the single-minded pursuit of values that result from faith helps each of us to transcend self-interest and opens each of us to perceive the call of God.

Practice patient-urgency

The strategy of firing up the energies of the spirit must include the double quality of patient-urgency. We must have patience in living faithfully those values that motivate us in the transformation of ourselves and of our world. However, we cannot be too patient! It is important, even urgent, that we bring about change. Patience will be required for the work is difficult. Too much patience thwarts the attaining of our goal. It is urgent that the work of transformation proceed. Too much urgency can hinder the calm, gradual transformation that is needed and can alienate others who need to be part of the transformation. So, an important energy of the spirit is the double quality of patient-urgency.

We need patient-urgency in coping with the normal pressures of everyday life. This takes patience but we cannot neglect the urgency to bring values to our world. In the Sermon on the Mount Jesus declares, "Blessed are those who mourn, for they shall be comforted," and "Blessed are the meek, for they will inherit the earth" (Matt 5:4-5). These are both strong qualities, both part of the patient-urgency we need. The former refers to those who undergo life's hardships and live patiently through oppression, domination, and abuse of their rights, while striving to be faithful to their values. The latter refers to those who accept life under God without complaint. These dedicated individuals strive with urgent commitment to respond to their calling while patiently enduring the problems such fidelity brings. Such individuals are in tune with their essential calling and remain committed to it in spite of the domination of evil around them. Patient-urgency is a prophetical stance in a world that often loses values that matter.

It is, of course, urgent that we have a clearly focused impact on our world. Left to ourselves we can drift into mediocrity and then into periods without the values we had felt called to uphold. Our world easily slides into situations where evil seems more dominant than goodness. Our faith-filled experiences of God's loving challenge call us to dedicate ourselves to our own and to the world's transformation. We are challenged to build lives anew on values that help us be the best we are capable of being. It is urgent that this transformation progress. So, we need to live daily, motivated by a sense of patient-urgency.

Enjoy life

As people of faith, we should be naturally optimistic and enthusiastic about our lives, and convinced that they be full of joy. Unfortunately, some people find their joy in personal pleasure and self-satisfaction or in a sense of achievement beyond that of others around them. We find joy and happiness in making a difference to our own and to other people's lives and in giving ourselves to the appreciation of values beyond the normal horizons of life. We should enjoy doing good, being good, and experiencing ultimate goodness.

We find joy and delight in the ordinary events of life. We can be fully present to people and to events, appreciating them and enjoying them as gifts that they are to us from a gracious God. Our faith gives us a new perspective on life. Sharing is more important to us than competition with others. We can delight in others' achievements rather than comparing them to our own. We value the contributions of everyone and reject the typical mutual blame found in so much of contemporary society. A positive outlook with optimism and enthusiasm brings about joy. People of faith should enjoy life.

When we are filled with joy we are also peacemakers, and that is one of the reasons why this energy of the spirit is so important. In a world of hatred, polarization, discrimination, and deliberate hurt, we, as people energized by joy, can bring about peacefulness in ourselves, in others around us, and in that part of society we can influence. Having stretched beyond the normal horizons of life we encountered a vision of the human community living in love and peace, and we now daily strive to make that hope a reality.

We meet many people who always seem burdened with problems that life brings them, or with themselves and their poor self-concept, or with others' lack of respect for them, and so on. So much of our experience is of a joyless world, but we have a mission to spread joy. It is an energy of our spirit.

Be generous

Every experience in our spiritual lives is an experience of God's generosity towards us, reminding us that we must live with generosity towards others. Generosity implies treating others with goodness, abundant support, and prodigious gestures of loving service. When we are generous, we move the focus away from ourselves to emphasize the importance of others.

Generosity can sometimes appropriately refer to financial support for the needy, those who a have suffered from natural disasters, the homeless, and the unemployed. This practical way of helping those in need is a fine quality of good human beings everywhere. However, generosity is essentially about self-gift, sharing with others our time when they need it; our words to support, encourage, console, and motivate; our presence to people in compassionate care, understanding, and love; our forgiveness to those who may have done us harm. Generosity means giving not taking. It is a gesture from those who have to those who have not, provided we always appreciate that generosity is mutual. We are all always the haves and have nots at the same time, for those who give receive by their giving.

Generosity is an energy of our inner spirit and is part of who we are. We evidence it in all situations. Thus, we live generously with close friends and family, as much as with strangers, coworkers, and the needy. We show friends and family love without measure. In dealing with them we strive to choose the most loving thing to do, to forgive abundantly, to show limitless understanding, and to be magnanimous in our relationships. As we live with generosity, we are daily becoming who we are capable of being, for generosity is creative of our personalities.

This energy of the spirit leads us to have a benevolent attitude to all. We learn to wish others well even before we know them. This anticipatory benevolence towards all, based as it is on our experience of God's approach toward us, contributes towards mutual understanding and respect, dialogue, collaboration, and community building. Generosity is a wonderful energy of the human spirit and should not be left to chance or show itself only sporadically. We need to deliberately channel this quality.

Show compassion

Compassion is one of the most beautiful qualities that we can extend to others. If we train ourselves to make this an intentional response, we draw out an energy of the spirit that can transform society. Compassion means "to suffer with," and it describes being with others in the intimacy of their pain. Compassion means feeling the way others do in their suffering, enduring the pain with them, and supporting them in mutual efforts. Compassion is a healing service to others, journeying with them through the difficulties of their lives.

Our contemporary world is no different than it has been in other times, it gives little evidence of compassion. Rather, it is often characterized by selfishness, greed, and abuse of others. So many seem to choose dominant, hateful approaches to others. When we show compassion, the evil of this world cannot deal with it. They certainly cannot oppose it for it is clearly a genuine quality, at the heart of humanity. In fact, evil people in our world do not know what to do with compassion. They see it, silently appreciate it, sometimes mock it as weakness, but can never oppose it.

We show compassion to ourselves and our failures, to others in their many needs, to the world when the environment is abused. There is so much pain, loss, sickness, and abuse. People are marginalized and discriminated against for all kinds of reasons. Our compassion needs to be practical and implies fighting for justice. Ours has to be more than a believed-in compassion, it has to be real. This will imply not being afraid to show our feelings and emotions as we suffer together with those in pain. We also need to identify the causes of pain, to seek alleviation in the short term where possible, and to pursue solutions for situations that bring so much torment and suffering.

Sometimes there are no solutions to the pain people feel. It might be a terminal illness that has no end except further pain and death. It could be the loss of loved ones, tragically taken in war or in a natural disaster. There is really nothing we can do. God does not act in the way human beings think God should act. We need to be together in mutual compassion faced with a mystery we do not understand, trusting in God's love that we cannot see, believing in a divine plan we cannot understand. We strive to be together, to console each other, to sustain each other's commitment, and to let each other know our love.

Live in touch with tradition

A spiritual experience always includes a sense of community, for in the transforming experience one sees a realm beyond this one that portrays God's plan for the world—a plan for salvation in a loving community. But we also see our experience as a point in history and know we belong to a tradition of God's love and of the human struggle to respond. This awareness that we are a part of a community and that we stand at a point in history with a past and a future can energize us in our responses to the challenges of spiritual growth.

We have a history, we have connections with ancestors who have lived, loved, survived, and grown, and we can appreciate them as models to be imitated and sometimes to be avoided. Some were ordinary figures and others even heroic. They are an integral part of our own lives. There are also those who will come into existence in the future and who are already linked to us. We look in both directions and sense our responsibility for our vision of life, linked to the past and maybe creative of the future.

Our connections are not only with family members but with humanity in its struggles to solve the most fundamental questions concerning the meaning of life. We learn what it means to be human and pass our awareness on to others. We welcome the great figures of our past, saints and mystics, who teach, inspire, motivate, and enlighten us on our current pursuit of the journey they already took. Certainly we are part of a communion of humanity; call it a communion of saints if you wish. Living aware of this need to maintain traditions draws out values of the spirit in our contemporary struggles.

In this context, community expressions of faith in God can support, nurture, and strengthen our dedication. Belief systems formulated by others can help, even though they cannot substitute for our personal experiences of faith. Even religions with their awkwardness and graciousness, with their frequent corruption and constant challenge, with their sporadic causes and perennial standards—such communities can help us, as we become integral parts of a community of shared faith. Preserving a sense of tradition can be a fruitful energy of our spirit.

Key reflections:

- Think about your own vocation and purpose in life.
- Are you faithful in pursuing the values that you are convinced motivate you?
- Reflect on how you can be a more generous person.
- Develop an awareness of how you are intimately connected to others in community.

Action items:

➢ Establish a simple method to guarantee you make decisions based on your faith-filled experience.
➢ Examine your current life at home and at work to see if you can be more dedicated to a balance of patience and urgency.
➢ Deliberately bring joy to someone else today.

➢ Specify who needs your compassion and how you can respond.

Focus questions for one's personal journal.

Develop a sense of call

>   Do you feel a sense of call or vocation? For what?
>
>   What qualities do you bring to this?

Discern before deciding

>   What is discernment?
>
>   How do you practice it?

Be single-minded

>   Are you clear about your sense of purpose in life?
>
>   Does your purposefulness ever become arrogance?

Practice patient-urgency

>   Do you need more patience or more urgency?
>
>   What difficulties do you encounter as a result of your purposeful fidelity?

Enjoy life

>   Where do you find your greatest joy?
>
>   How do you bring joy to other people?

Be generous

>   Do you think you are generous?
>
>   To whom do you show generosity and to whom ought you to show it?

Show compassion

>   Describe why you think you are a compassionate person.
>
>   Are you compassionate toward yourself? How?

Live in touch with tradition

>   What role does community play in your spiritual life?
>
>   Do you have a sense of belonging to a community with a history and tradition?

Planning for Strategy Four: Firing up the energies of the soul.

1. List three important goals that will enable you to fire up the energies of your soul.

2. What are your personal gifts that could help you attain these goals?

3. Specify any weaknesses that could stunt these energies of the soul.

4. What can you do in the short term to achieve these goals?

5. How will you achieve these resolutions?

6. When will you do this?

7. Will you do this alone or with others? With whom?

8. How will you evaluate how successful you have been?

Topics for group discussion or sharing.

1. How would each of you describe your own most significant energies of the soul?
2. Which important energies should be added to those listed in the chapter?
3. What are some important group or community energies that merit emphasis?
4. Which energies of the soul result from baptism?

STRATEGY FIVE
REMEMBER SUFFERING

See links between suffering and faith

Our experiences of God's love include an appreciation of being part of a community called to love. When faced with suffering we must react in a particular way in order to show we are Christian. It is not just that we confront "the problem of suffering"; but more importantly we become aware that how we deal with suffering authenticates our spiritual commitment. We accept our own personal suffering as part of the human condition, and we appreciate how much we need others' support in times of suffering. We must live differently because of suffering.

Early Christians, reflecting on Jesus' life and teachings, could have chosen from among a host of symbols and teachings something to remind them of the Lord's life and work. They chose the crucifix, an image both of humans inflicting suffering and at the same time of the redemptive value of suffering when linked to love. Then for their primary ritual to celebrate until the Lord's return, they chose the ritual re-living of the Lord's passion, both in the Easter Triduum and in the weekly celebration of the Lord's Supper. This memorializing of suffering gives a special authority to suffering in Christianity. Moreover, this responsibility is not just to the pastoral alleviation of suffering with charity, the corporal works of mercy, the founding of hospitals, the roles of religious orders, chaplains, and so on. Rather, how we think about suffering and how we deal with it in our own lives and in the lives of others transforms us into compassionate human beings whose lives are motivated by real faith.

A Christian lives in hope in spite of all the brokenness around us. In fact, our spiritual lives assure us that our approach to suffering makes us identify with the suffering, compassionate Lord. In suffering we long for redemption and yearn for wholeness. Suffering always aligns itself with hope for release and for healing. As Christians we appreciate suffering endured for someone else and the power of suffering linked to love.

Our world is anything but perfect. We are surrounded by human suffering, much of it caused by human beings, part of it unanswered because some self-centered people have other selfish priorities. The common experience of suffering connects human beings from all over the world. Common responses to suffering would bring us even closer together. Unfortunately, many inflict suffering in God's name, and their blasphemy destroys their own and others' faith.

So, if our experience of God's transforming love in our lives means anything to us, it must imply a call to ongoing transformation of ourselves and of our world. It means confronting suffering. First, we try to accept the mystery of suffering in life; there are certain aspects of suffering about which we can do nothing. God is different than what we think God ought to be. Second, suffering is often linked to the problem of evil and cries out for redemptive love. Third, how we deal with suffering transforms us or dehumanizes us. Fourth, suffering is connected to faith; it is a characteristic of a fallen world that we believe needs redemption. Finally, Jesus teaches that confronting suffering is faith's proof of hope and love.

Remembering suffering is an important strategy for people of faith. Dealing with it shows where the values of our mind and heart lie—focused on self or on others. It shows we move from self-centeredness to self-transcendence; that we have truly understood the nature of our call to spiritual growth. Also focusing on suffering reminds us that life is really about healing and redemption, the removal of undesirable obstacles, and the search for wholeness. Suffering can be physical, psychological, moral, or spiritual. Healing will include a sense of well-being, restoration of human dignity, and clarification of the meaning of life and of death.

Remember suffering

As people committed to spiritual growth, we cannot live without remembering suffering. This remembering must be specific and not some vague recollection of human emptiness, brokenness, and hatred. We need to remember our own sufferings—specific episodes or situations in life that caused us pain. Our pain could come from sickness, loss of love, problems in employment, destruction of our self-concept, failure to live up to our own calling. It could come from natural disasters, evils of war, injustices of others, marginalization, and so on. We should think about each specific event and the suffering it brought or continues to bring. We think of other people, individuals and groups, who we personally know or of whom we have heard, and we think deeply about their suffering—its causes, how they felt, what response or lack of response they received from others, what we have learnt or failed to learn from their pain. People could be victims of oppression or neglect, objects of others' violence—physical, psychological, financial, legal, or political. They might be those who are bought or sold in human trafficking, slaves for sexual perversion or for cheap labor or even for body parts.

We particularly remember the sufferings of the innocent, immersed in pain for no reason. What are the causes of this unjustified suffering, what role does humanity play in this, is it part of the structural sin of the human community. We think about the victims of war—displaced, used as pawns, violated. We remember those who suffer because of others' irresponsibility and lack of ethics—their savings stolen by greedy criminals, their homes destroyed too easily in natural disasters because contractors cut corners. We remember the sick, elderly, children—innocent sufferers in marital problems, power conflicts, victims of drought and starvation. We remember and ask why, what can be done about it, how can things change?

Our world does not like to remember suffering, and sometimes we ourselves pass over it. We say we must bring closure and move on. But we need to savor suffering, whether in our own lives or in others', both individually and institutionally. I believe we must make people confront suffering. It is important to me as part of Christian dedication to interrupt the peaceful and deliberate ignoring of others' suffering. To suggest that the happiness and painless existence of a few at the top will trickle down to bring happiness and the alleviation of suffering for the poor, sick, helpless masses is itself an example of the sickness that infects society. In fact, the alleviation of suffering is blocked by sinful, selfish acts of individuals for sure, but, the major blocks to remembering suffering come from attitudes that, while immoral, have become the normal order of the day. These disordered positions become part of our culture, our normal way of viewing things. They are rationalized, justified, and even religiously supported—all efforts to anaesthetize us against suffering. Remembering suffering challenges us to come up with new priorities in our way of thinking.

We actively and courageously remember suffering. We can never identify suffering only with some unfortunate others, for there is suffering in everyone's life. Clearly, some suffer immensely and unjustly, but suffering is part of the human condition, and we can all relate to it—it is part of who we are. Even those who inflict suffering on others are sick and in need of healing. Certainly, it takes courage to remember suffering. The horrors of Auschwitz were inflicted by human beings, mainly Christians, who made us see the total moral depravity to which human beings can fall. Recent natural disasters with entire cities destroyed sees much of the blame going to builders, planners, enforcers, who failed in their duties, causing death and destruction and revealing the consequences of cheating. We have witnessed enormous greed in business and finance that has ruined the lives of millions while the guilty perpetrators walk away with the wealth they have stolen from their clients. It takes courage to remember suffering for some memories can be dangerous. When we look at suffering it can be a shocking experience, reminding us of what humanity can become. This frightening experience can change us from being selfish to selfless. It can challenge us to think about ourselves as we stand before God and about the true values of humanity. Faced with the horrors of suffering we are called to live the values of our faith.

There are three components of dedicated believers' approach to suffering. First, we remember suffering, our own and others, especially the dangerous life-changing memories of suffering. Second, we commit ourselves to solidarity with those who suffer. In other words, we make the daily effort to see life from the victim's point of view, from the victim's struggles for hope. We must truly participate in others' suffering. Third, we listen to the stories of others' sufferings, so we can remember them and then act with the eyes of the victim focused on us. Memory of suffering, solidarity in suffering, and listening to the stories of those who suffer are three tasks we can practice as people of faith to help us constantly remember suffering. However, our memories must have a purpose; they must move us to action. Remembering suffering can transform our lives, bringing a spirit of humility, solidarity, compassion, and community. If we fail to remember suffering we can become arrogant, hard-hearted, selfish, and inhuman.

Respond to suffering

People of spiritual dedication, caught up in suffering can draw on their inner strength, endurance, hope, and love, as they long for redemptive healing. Their hearts go out to others who suffer, they feel a profound sadness for those who cause it, and they admire those who live peacefully through suffering. They can sense how good the absence of suffering can be and determine to remove it from the lives of others.

Suffering is anything that negatively affects well-being, and there is no satisfactory explanation for all situations. Suffering is linked to the problem of evil, the mystery of life, and the incomprehensibility of God. The first response to suffering by people of faith in God's love is to be dumbfounded—shocked that there can be suffering in a world created by God's love. Being dumbfounded at suffering is an important response, and we should not immediately seek excuses for God's ways with the world. Rather, we need to be conscious of the horrors of suffering, and while we must later respond in action, we need above all to face how wrong suffering is.

Once we adequately realize how terrible the situation of suffering is, we need to identify precisely what it is. We need to name the pain. This diagnostic response is one of discernment, carefully judging what is causing the suffering. This includes reflecting on contemporary evils found in economics, healthcare, politics, and elsewhere—situations that are blatantly wrong and unjust, but continue in contemporary societies, bringing suffering to so many. Many contemporary institutions and social structures are themselves the causes of suffering to many. They never become just by their charities and contributions to causes; they are inherently unjust and need to be changed. As people of faith, we must face the realities of the modern causes of socially inflicted pain.

Responding to suffering means a new view of the world and of what it means to be human. Suffering always calls out for healing, for it just seems wrong. When suffering is inflicted deliberately or results as a consequence of one's self-centered choices it is always contrary to humanity. Responding means a conversion—a change of heart, a new outlook on life. As people of faith, we look to the basic values we hold as a result of our faith-filled encounter. From these basic values there emerges our purpose in life. This philosophy of life gives rise to a sense of purpose and destiny. All these elements together form our vision of life—a vision that sees suffering as an aberration, whether it is our own suffering or someone else's. Responding must eventually lead to action, but first we must take a stance against all suffering, making sure this new outlook resulting from conversion leads us to think and live differently.

No matter how bad the situation is, so many people, including Christians, never respond. Spirituality calls for conversion, and this different outlook on life leads to a series of convictions, evidenced in our attitudes to the world. Wherever suffering occurs we must yearn to respond. If suffering comes from sickness, loss, natural disasters, our hearts should immediately go out in compassion. There is no suffering to which we can be insensitive. We can even judge ourselves as to how human, Christian, or faith-filled we are by our response to suffering. We must live with deep convictions against all forms of abuse, all manifestations of domination, every sign of violence. We should always be on the lookout for any abuse of power, manipulation of others, and unjust treatment in healthcare, finance, banking, politics, working conditions, law, and religion. Suffering, whatever its causes, is a red light to people of spiritual depth. We immediately stop, assess, make judgments, and view the world differently.

Attitudes to suffering have a special place in human growth, for our approach to suffering makes us more human or less human. So, responding is intimately linked to who we are and who we can become. Our response is part of our spirituality. Having experienced

God's love, we must live to share it and fight against any abuse or absence of it. This implies confronting suffering with a vision of faith. We prove our commitment in hope, and hope is only real when it endures through suffering. Without the test of suffering, hope becomes empty words. Our attitudes to suffering are not only focused through faith and hope, but particularly because we believe and hope in love. Love guides our approach to suffering at every stage.

Answer the call to action

We respond to suffering first and foremost with a new vision and understanding of the importance of confronting suffering to prove faith, hope, and love. However, we must then move to a call for action. When human effort can contribute, there is no excuse for not doing so. Sometimes, there is suffering we cannot change but at least we can compassionately help to transform such suffering, uniting the pain with the suffering Christ. Likewise, some suffering is neither reformable nor transformable, and then we can only offer the faith solution of active endurance. Always we approach these various situations with solidarity in suffering. We can use various contributing remedies—medicine and psychology, prayer and rituals, educational and spiritual ministries. We reform, transform, or endure with the aid of sacramental, charismatic, pastoral, and spiritual skills.

Pastoral care of those who suffer shows forth our compassion. In addition, we must align our behavior with our values and become actively involved in removing situations that cause suffering. First, we can actively and deliberately withhold support from individuals or organizations that cause suffering or do nothing to alleviate suffering even though they could. So, we can withhold support from unethical organizations that cause suffering. Some groups that support war and those who finance them, some banking systems and practices that discriminate, some healthcare and pharmaceutical companies whose policies of pricing and of withholding help lead to suffering, some political subgroups who negatively affect the poor and unfortunate—we can target all these for inflicting suffering on others. Current injustices in business, healthcare, education, and law are the same as they have been for years, and we can actively oppose leaders who do harm or do nothing.

We can also become more socially and politically involved in order to work to reduce suffering. We can support movements that challenge injustice and alleviate suffering. Thus, we can support movements for women's justice, healthcare for the poor at home and throughout the world, movements for children's welfare, safety, and education, movements that support victims of all kinds of abuse. We must work for what is not only legal, but what is fair, what is just, and what is in keeping with a vision based on faith.

The call to action will always include pastoral care, wide-ranging charity, active involvement, and collaborative efforts of movements for social response. Above all, people who wish to deepen their spiritual lives will work to institutionalize change. Religions with their social teachings can help, so too can the lonely voices of activists, many of whom have spearheaded change in our own generation. We can use the power of the ballot box, the choice of firms in which to invest, the banks with whom we are willing to do business, and the churches we are willing to attend. Every time we relate to organizations we can ask what have you done to remove suffering. Do any of your policies or practices lead to suffering for others? We must let it be known that we will categorically reject any organization that does not share our faith-filled values of Christian love.

As people of faith, we realize that suffering is closely linked to our faith. We remember the passion of Christ and the passion of all those who suffer for whatever reason. We courageously recall our memories of suffering, especially the life challenging and life changing dangerous memories. We dedicate ourselves to respond first with a new vision of reality in which we give importance to understanding, confronting, and alleviating suffering. Then, we engage in a call to action to institutionalize change.

Key reflections:

- Think about the causes of suffering and whether you are the cause of suffering for anyone else.
- Reflect on whether there is anything in your life and work that causes suffering to others.

- What would be the most dangerous memory of suffering in your experience?
- When you read of suffering in the paper or listen to events on TV make sure you give time to reflect on what you see.

Action items:

➤ Remind yourself often of other people's suffering.
➤ This week find several ways of being in solidarity with people who are suffering.
➤ Identify organizations with which you have contact that are the causes of suffering to others and plan to respond.
➤ Examine whether your political positions and voting record further suffering or alleviate it.

Focus questions for one's personal journal.

See links between suffering and faith
How do you live differently because of suffering?
Why do Christians memorialize suffering?
Describe how you see the power of suffering linked to love.
How are you personally linked to suffering?
Can you confront suffering? How?
How do you heal personal suffering?
Remember suffering
What suffering do you remember most?
Do you remember other people's suffering?
Can you challenge other people's forgetfulness of suffering?
Describe socially inflicted suffering where you live.
How do you approach suffering?
Respond to suffering
Describe how your heart goes out to those who suffer.
Why is there suffering in a world created by God's love?
Name the suffering in your life.
How have you taken a stance against suffering?
What are the new kinds of suffering inflicted by the society in which you live?
How is responding to suffering a part of your faith?
Answer the call to action
Is there suffering around you that you neglect to respond to?

What do you do to confront organizations that cause suffering?

Describe how you are socially and politically involved to remove suffering.

What have you done to institutionalize reactions to suffering?

What have you learnt about suffering by reflecting on the passion of Christ?

Planning for Strategy Five: Remembering suffering.

1. List three important tasks that would help you to remember and confront suffering.

2. What are your personal gifts that could help you attain these goals?

3. Specify any weaknesses that could stunt your remembering suffering.

4. What can you do in the short term to achieve these goals?

5. How will you achieve these resolutions?

6. When will you do this?

7. Will you do this alone or with others? With whom?

8. How will you evaluate how successful you have been?

Topics for group discussion or sharing.

1. Discuss how each member of the group sees the links between suffering and faith.
2. Let each one present the most dangerous memory of suffering that he or she has experienced.
3. What can the group do to respond together to suffering?
4. Reflect on those aspects of suffering that one can do nothing about.

STRATEGY SIX
KEEP HOPE ALIVE

Live in light of the future

Hope is the most fundamental attitude of Christianity. We have faith in what we hope for, and without hope our faith becomes empty statements. For us, the past is not determinative of the way we live in the present, the future is. In fact, the main question facing human beings is what will happen at the end of life. How we view the end revolutionizes how we deal with the present. Hope is a way of approaching the present because of what we believe about the future. Personally, I find the present to be very oppressive and think I must focus on the future as a source of hope. So, hope is not unconnected with the present, rather it challenges us to transform the present as an anticipation of the future. Thus, keeping hope alive is an important strategy for people who seek to deepen their spiritual lives.

Our experience of God's love is an anticipation of union with God beyond the normal realm of life. What we hope for is the fullness of the life we experienced in faith. Faith then challenges us to live in light of the future we hope for. Thus, hope gives rise to the duty to work in the present for peace, justice, human development, love, and community. Living the consequences of our faith-experience and anticipating the consequences of our hope challenge us to transform our world according to God's vision for humanity—a program of action for us all in personal and institutional renewal. Hope has too often been a forgotten virtue, a discarded energy of the human spirit, and a lost dimension of life, whereas for each of us, it ought to be the most important motivating force to transform the present.

Hope deals with the ultimate meaning of life. We cannot reduce hope to the small, often mutually exclusive daily hopes that each of us may have. Hope implies knowledge about the future to which God calls us, appreciation of history and the yearnings of humanity, awareness of sin and human weakness, and acknowledgement of death and human longings beyond death. It is not the minor hopes of each day but a vision of life with God.

People of hope must also keep their feet on the ground and make sure their vision changes the realities of the present in politics, social developments, justice, community development, and human fulfillment. We contribute to the realization of our vision of hope in daily activity based on decisions that anticipate the future. These decisions form part of our ongoing conversion in interaction with our contemporary world. Our hope is no longer focused exclusively on the afterlife, but nowadays as people of faith we have hope for our own world. We are not alone in this task; hope is an expression of a community striving to change our world for the better, and thus bring about God's promise for the whole human community.

Living in light of the future means working with others to develop a trusting environment in which we can dedicate ourselves to the common vision of hope. It means supporting each other, appreciating everyone's contribution to the shared vision of community. Part of working together is to energize each one's dedication through mutual inspiration with enthusiasm, joy, and optimism. This common commitment to transform our world in hope includes deliberately making shared decisions based on the hoped-for future. This will include courage and a spirit of daring to strive for goals others think unattainable. Living in light of the future, all empower each other, delegate whenever possible, and always celebrate each other's gifts.

Be people of hope

We can keep hope alive by emphasizing four ways of living our hope. We evidence hope in living the tasks of a prophet, a mystic, a charismatic, and a healer. A prophet focuses on the authenticity and integrity of the vision, challenging others to change now because of the future vision. The mystic stresses the understanding that emerges from a profound faith-filled experience. The charismatic celebrates the many mutually authenticating gifts of the community—gifts that anticipate the future vision. The healer emphasizes our hope for universal redemption and personal and organizational transformation in hope.

As prophets we attempt to tell the community how they ought to live in the present in light of the authentic goals of humanity and the call of God. Prophets are hope-filled individuals of exceptional moral qualities, lonely incorruptible people of faith who have the courage to do what is right no matter the consequences. They challenge injustice, give encouragement in trials, and call for renewal and transformation. They bring the future vision of hope to bear on concrete, contemporary decision-making; they are visionaries of how things should be. Prophetical ministry is part of the vocation of every person of faith—to challenge the present in light of the desired and hoped-for future.

One who appreciates the transcendent in life is a mystic. We strive to be everyday mystics amidst our busy, involved, and productive lives, but above all else we are also people of interiority and hope. We build interactions exclusively on what we have experienced of justice, compassion, respect, community, mutuality, and love. We have also journeyed within our own hearts and experienced the darkness that comes with religious experience— discovering that our God of hope often acts differently than we expected God would. Thus, we must undergo transformation and move beyond normal horizons to discover a new calling, a new sense of ourselves, and a new confidence in our role in the world. We do this primarily through a profound spiritual experience that motivates us in all we do.

Charismatics are people with special gifts that they use for the building and encouraging of others in community and in organizations. Called to be charismatics, we also appreciate that other people are gifted and form part of a gifted, charismatic community. These gifts anticipate and can bring into reality the vision of hope. Genuine charismatics have extraordinary qualities but are always humble, serve the community, and inspire it to its future calling. Charisms can be long-term, are frequently short-term, and all benefit the community. So, we appreciate how our own and other people's gifts can build up a vision of hope.

Being people of hope and striving for healing are two aspects of the same reality. People of hope heal themselves, others, and organizational structures, restoring harmony, wellness, and healthy interactions. As people of hope, we constantly ask what individuals and organizations would be like if all were functioning well. Then, healing begins with the mind and heart, values, vision, mission, and structures.

We live out our mission as people of hope by focusing on these four tasks—four aspects of the personality of an individual of hope: to be a prophetical, mystical, charismatic, and healing force in our world.

Cultivate hope

One of the fundamental attitudes that helps us cultivate hope is optimism by which we show others we have a positive view of reality, expect new developments, and anticipate good things happening. Our optimism is linked to joy and enthusiasm—qualities that are infectious in dealing with others and in encouraging them to look forward in hope. This optimistic approach is supported by a sense of wonder. When we look at the world, we feel inspired by events of daily life, delight in the vision of hope, and savor the goodness of God. Optimistic people are men and women of gratitude—they appreciate they are part of something wonderful.

We can cultivate hope by a spirit of openness and challenge to our future vision of hope. Openness means listening, learning, welcoming change, appreciating diversity, communicating generously, and welcoming the gifts of others. In this way we can welcome new ideas and become ready for the contributions that others can bring. To maintain openness we have to assure freedom to all around us, letting them say what they wish and be who they choose to be. We can help people be free from their own inhibitions, from prejudice, from routines that block growth, and from apathy. Together with all around us, we can be open to the future God plans for us.

Part of cultivating hope includes tapping what lies deep within us. Each of us can enrich our appreciation of the vision of hope through creativity. This can energize and strengthen our commitment to keep hope alive; confirming that what we hope for is also linked to the deepest gifts within us. When challenged by hope we often have to think differently, act differently, and be different— always reaching for new creative possibilities, new insights, and a new openness to the transcendent. We must not only tap the inner potentials of our own spirit, but those of others too. Through dialogue and collaboration we can search for shared values in hope. This means approaching others with mutual respect, friendship, and love, capitalizing on their creative contributions to a vision of hope.

It is love that allows us to treat others in light of hope. With humility, trust, and reconciliation, we can work together for the shared vision for which we all yearn. Love begins with simple gestures of respect, concern, compassion, kindness, gentleness, and patience. These are qualities that also facilitate a community of hope, and that community then becomes humanizing, caring, trusting, and supportive. Love cultivates hope through establishing solidarity, friendship, and appreciating a shared vision. So, we can cultivate hope through genuine community. We can cultivate our common vision of hope by acknowledging and developing our shared core values. These are the values that are integral to the future vision for which we long, and we live in a loving community of hope with a passion for the same values.

Cultivating hope is not easy because others will consider us different, even outside the normal approach to life. So, we will each need a good self-concept, confidence, and courage. Clearly, people of hope have an outsider mentality that others will criticize. Moreover, people of hope will need to avoid arrogance and self-righteousness that often come with being different. Criticism comes quickly when exploratory hopes come to nothing. There will be failures, but we must not lose courage. People of hope need to be resilient and be satisfied with small incremental steps in the realization of a vision of hope—which is always beyond our grasp. Optimism, openness, creativity, love, along with a sense of mystery, a spirit of freedom, genuine collaboration, and resilience can all help us cultivate hope.

Practice hope

Hope is a gift that transforms everything we do. At the same time we can nurture and enrich it by a series of daily practices. A first practice that can keep hope alive is to mourn its absence in our daily lives. We must face so much negative news every day—wars, natural disasters, oppression, all kinds of injustice, immorality, and inactivity on the part of people who could help to change our world. We are immersed in a world without hope and we must mourn its loss. It is painful to think about our depressing world, and the pain just stays with us, tearing at our hearts. Savoring the loss of hope is a helpful practice that helps us keep things in perspective and value how much we long for hope.

A second practice is to reflect so that we train ourselves to appreciate what lies beyond the normal sphere of life. We must think about serious issues, learn to meditate in order to discover deeper levels of meaning in events of our lives, and contemplate signs of God's presence to us. As people of hope, we need to make connections to transcendent values, appreciate the plan of God, and draw conclusions on the importance of love, justice, equality, interdependence, and goodness. Every day there are moments of insight, profound experiences that lead us to appreciate connections to a life beyond this one. Unconditional love, utter beauty and harmony, selfless dedication, endurance of suffering, and similar values lead us to ask why people evidence these qualities or why do we. There has to be a reason beyond the present in convictions regarding a vision of hope.

A further practice that helps us keep hope alive is to focus on love; to work to unlock the potentials of our own hearts and other peoples' hearts too. Hope requires real friendship, love, and community among all who share a common vision. Love begins with practical manifestations of understanding, welcoming ideas, sharing deeply personal feelings, giving and receiving emotional support. In the loving community for which we hope, members respect each other, welcome each other's gifts, value each other's ideas, share a common vision, and work for a common mission. Thus, love makes our faith and hope real, moves us away from self-centeredness to self-transcendence, and anticipates the loving community life for which we hope. We daily make choices based on the most loving thing to do, we choose reconciliation as a priority, and strategize to develop union and community as goals of our daily efforts.

Many men and women today live so sure of themselves, selfishly and arrogantly stressing immediate gratification in total disregard of others. An important practice of hope is to interrupt this short-sighted self security and challenge people to a more integrated vision of life and of hope. We must instill doubt and uncertainty in their superficial convictions and raise anxious questions regarding an unknown and unfamiliar future. People of hope ask questions no one else does, theological and philosophical questions, regarding purpose in life, God's plan for humanity, the goal of human growth, the needs of the common good, and so on. They can also ask how we can anticipate the future for which we long, how can our present decisions contribute to what we seek, are we motivated by the past or the present instead of the future. Interrupting comfortable self-satisfying mediocrity and asking questions no one else does can help ourselves and others to focus on hope.

A further practice to keep hope alive is to develop in ourselves and in others a new sense of commitment. People of hope enthusiastically commit themselves to attain the future vision that inspires and attracts them. This is more than the regular commitment found in professionals who do a great job. Commitment to transform our world becomes part of one's spirituality. This commitment is relational—it includes others. It is synergetic, fusing together a shared commitment greater than the component parts. It is a commitment based on mutuality—everyone inspires and is inspired, motivates and is motivated, heals and is healed, leads and is led. The commitment of a community of hope helps realize the vision for which people of spiritual dedication strive.

Key reflections:

- Think about your experience of faith and ask how it ought to change your life in the present.
- Try to appreciate the gifts of those around you, in family and at work.
- Examine whether you are an optimistic, joyful, and enthusiastic person. If not, why not?

- Would other people consider you an outsider? How are you different because of your hope?

Action items:

➤ This week, deliberately do something that you have never done before that anticipates your vision of hope.

➤ Identify what you can do to be prophetical, mystical, charismatic, and healing for others.

➤ Spend a little time reflecting on the absence of hope in our contemporary world.

➤ Next week, find a way of interrupting the shortsighted complacency of some around you.

Focus questions for one's personal journal.

Live in light of the future

What do you think will happen at the end of life?

Describe the connections between faith and hope.

How does hope affect your daily life?

What do you hope for this world?

How does your own hope relate to other people's hope?

Be a person of hope

Describe ways you keep hope alive.

Do other people see you as a prophet?

Describe how you can be an everyday mystic.

What are your special gifts or charisms?

When does hope have a healing impact on others?

Cultivate hope

Do you think you are optimistic?

In what ways are you open to the future?

Describe the potential of your inner spirit.

What have you learnt about hope from other people?

Describe when you are an outsider.

Practice hope

When is hope absent from your life?

Do you spend to more time thinking about serious issues or trivial ones?

Describe a loving community of which you are a part.

Who do you find to be arrogant and self-assured? Do you have these tendencies?

What does commitment mean to you and has it changed in recent years?

Planning for Strategy Six: Keeping hope alive.

1. List three important things you can do to keep hope alive.

2. What are your personal gifts that could help you attain these goals?

3. Specify any weaknesses that could stunt your efforts to keep hope alive.

4. What can you do in the short term to achieve these goals?

5. How will you achieve these resolutions?

6. When will you do this?

7. Will you do this alone or with others? With whom?

8. How will you evaluate how successful you have been?

Topics for group discussion or sharing.

1. How does your understanding of the future impact the way you live in the present?
2. Let each one describe how he or she conveys to others that he or she is a person of hope.
3. How does each of you maintain a spirit of hope?
4. What can the group do to help people out of their hopelessness?

STRATEGY SEVEN
DO GOOD FOR OTHERS

Focus every day on others

The person's journey to God is a journey towards union with God and community with others. It begins with the invitation of God, moves through repentance and hope, and then culminates in charity. The response of the person seeking spiritual growth is a generous and effective dedication to work with and for others, to become a servant to all, and to put his or her talents at the service of others. Christians emphasize a sense of community in order to be an authentic presence of Christ's followers today. It implies working with others to make Christ's love visible in the world.

The most fundamental action of people dedicated to spiritual growth is the movement away from self-centeredness to focus on God and on others. This is integral to human maturity and to the maturing of one's spiritual life. It includes a letting go of selfishness and self-pity and calls for a confident and courageous growth with others. Focusing daily life on doing good to others is a wonderful way to attain one's own growth. Moving away from self-centeredness always implies self-transcendence and becomes a means of appreciating life beyond this one.

As we focus on others in our daily life, we emphasize simple human qualities that are also a noble part of being human—attitudes that are humanizing, caring, trusting, and supportive. Focusing on others requires tolerance of their differences, dialogue, forgiveness, and reconciliation. It means mutual respect, appreciation of each other's gifts and genuine solidarity. We can do so much good to others by allowing them to be themselves, living in interdependence and mutual esteem. We live in this way even when such qualities are not returned, for we can never be selfish because someone else is selfish.

For the person of faith, the welfare of others is as important as one's own. This includes concern for others' health and well-being, both material and spiritual. It means respecting and further pursuing others' rights within civil society or religion. It includes working for justice for those who find their justice threatened or totally destroyed. Engaging in the welfare of others calls each of us to delight in others' growth and advancement, even ahead of oneself. We lose when we compare ourselves to others, seeing who is best. Rather, we celebrate each other's progress, treasure others' advancement as much as our own, and appreciate diversity.

When we focus our daily life on others we learn the value of sharing our gifts and appreciate no one is complete in himself or herself. Rather we all need the courage to live aware that we are parts of a community and find our greater selves with others. Nowadays, we speak of fusion and synergy and appreciate that a dynamic interaction with others can produce more good than what we would otherwise be capable of as individuals. So, we focus daily life on others—it is the best way to facilitate our own growth, it is part of building Christian community, and it is a first step in doing good to others.

Bring out the best in others

People who take responsibility for their own spiritual lives should make a positive difference to other people's lives. If we respect the dignity of others we will empower them in whatever ways we can, thus releasing their human energy, talent, and dedication. We do not impose our views, vision, or priorities on others, but influence them to be the best they are capable of being. When in leadership positions, we must lead others to lead themselves. Making a difference to other people's lives requires humility; after all, we are not giving them something they did not have before, we are simply liberating the power within them, letting them become their true, gifted selves.

When we try to bring out the best in others we must strive to move them up in dignity and move them out in service to others. This means encouraging others to welcome change and the challenge that crisis can bring. Part of that response will be to help others appreciate their own basic values, enduring purpose, and mission in life. We can also train others to be visionaries; helping them to see what others do not, but also challenging them to look at things in a different way. Bringing out the best in others takes time and requires that people model the way and then coach others with care. This requires understanding, building connections, giving visibility and significant responsibilities to others. When we collaborate and challenge constructively we are effectively working toward shared values and mission.

We strive to bring to the fore the goodness of others, and this can start with creating a trusting environment which becomes the emotional glue that binds people together in a common endeavor. Trust includes respecting the competence of each other, highlighting others' positive contributions, and allowing people to move on after mistakes. Trust leads to sincere dialogue where people commit themselves to listen, to share honestly, to evaluate benevolently, and to strive for common good. Trust and dialogue produce collaboration which is not a way of doing things more effectively—even though it may well produce that result—but a way of being a community of faith more authentically. Collaboration requires peace of soul, freedom of spirit, prayer, and discernment. Leaders who wish to be collaborative seek mutual advice and consultation. Participation in decision-making, sharing authority, planning, and evaluating together are also essential.

Working together with other people so as to also bring out the best in them means sharing on three levels—intellectual, organizational, and personal, eventually integrating all three. Thus, such people give themselves in service to others so that other people feel empowered, trusted, and appreciated, whether acting individually or acting in teams. Working together will inevitably include conflict, but a person needs non-dominant responses, conflict resolution without arrogance. In this way, conflict can also draw out the best in others by becoming a situation of creative growth.

One of the finest ways of bringing out the best in others is to delegate responsibilities to them. This can be done in informal ways just as easily as in formal ways within a structure. When a person of dedication and spiritual commitment recognizes gifts in others, he or she wants to see them flourish, encourages them, and creates opportunities to see them develop. This person feels the need to get out of the way of other people's gifts, gives others credit wherever possible, invites them to take responsibility, and celebrates their successes.

Striving to bring out the best in others can never limit itself to respect, empowerment, trust, dialogue, collaboration, and delegation. While these are important, we yearn to share with others our enthusiasm for the profound experiences of faith, our vision of hope, and our commitment to believe in the power of love. We must humbly create an environment in which others can experience the transforming call of God. We can do this by sharing our own faith experiences, and showing connections to a realm beyond this one. Reflecting together on the challenges of life and revealing the powerful presence of God in our lives will energize us all.

Get involved

An extraordinary way of doing good is to get involved in enriching relationships. All around us we see dysfunctional relationships, whether in family, in society, in politics, or in religion. Then again, so many people seem stunted in developing their friendships, marriages, professional interactions, and so on. People who have an experience of faith in God's love know the importance of bringing forgiveness, healing, and reconciliation to relationships. We can show good will to all, never marginalize anyone, bridge differences, heal pain, and manifest caring attitudes to everyone. Those who have experienced God's love can show loving approaches to others. This effort will need to be practical, and such people will need to be trustworthy and live in peace, their language should never be hurtful. Moreover, they are willing to settle tensions and rivalries and avoid competitive attitudes. Above all, we must model healthy relationships, encouraging others to build mature relationships too.

Another way of giving to others and doing good is through volunteering, thereby using one's talents for the benefit of others with particular needs. We can volunteer locally in Church related activities or in one or other of the many social service groups found in every town. When involved in volunteering we need to be sure we are satisfying someone's real needs and not responding to our own need to be needed. By showing sensitivity, caring, compassion, interpersonal skills, and a sense of service, we can make our volunteering a serious professional commitment. We need to do something that capitalizes on our gifts and is a relevant involvement in others' needs. Likewise, if we need training we should get it; once involved we should plan, evaluate, and respond to new needs as they arise. What is important is that we sense a call to this kind of service, have genuine concern for others, and a strong desire to share our time and experience with others in need.

In spite of all the educational opportunities available to so many of us, there are always individuals or groups who think they have the right to make decisions for us. This is equally true in politics, business, healthcare, social services, and religion. Seldom do these people make decisions for our benefit or to reflect our values. So, a further way in which we can get involved in contemporary society is to make our voices heard. When people make decisions that do not reflect our values we should say so privately and publicly. We can demonstrate, join responses on the web, phone and e-mail our views, and withhold votes or financial support. As long as we let people do what they like in our names they will always continue to do so. We must put an end to the arrogant thwarting of our values by individuals who do not have any or clearly do not share ours. We need to make our voices heard and thereby make clear what we stand for and what we will not stand for.

Nowadays, getting involved means working for social change. The transformation of society rarely trickles down from high up in our political, social, business, or religious structures. The higher individuals rise in the organization the more they become committed to the structures of which they are parts. Rather, social change percolates up from small groups in which people insist on change and are willing to pay the price of change. This is where local movements of change begin their challenge to global issues. Striving for change in issues that relate to women and children, working conditions, immigration policy, healthcare reform, and so on, begins in small groups who gradually bring their commitment to bear on larger structures, thereby bringing about change. It is urgent that we bring about local change in these areas just mentioned, so that we can gradually impact global change. We have so many people, leaders and others, who live by injustice. They realize it, and they are dedicated to it as their only way of life. Good people cannot resolve all these issues, but should make sure they choose at least a couple of them to systematically confront, whether in church or civil society.

Getting involved in doing good cannot be left to chance, nor should it be merely sporadic. We need to prudently plan, maybe for six months at a time, choosing areas of need in which we can be effective, setting specific goals and intermediate objectives. People who do harm in our societies are meticulous in their planning, driven by selfishness, and at times motivated by greed or hatred. People of faith, inspired by a vision of love, must plan carefully to do the good they are called to do.

Work for peace

We all mourn the loss of peace in our world. When individuals or communities lack peace they cannot build up a life directed to God. We live immersed in violence with its abuse, fear, wars, ethnic cleansing, and environmental degradation. We have politicians and policies that fight against peace, business people who delight in the financial benefits of war, religions that blasphemously promote hatred and destruction, and churches focused in on themselves. There is violence in our unjust judicial systems, in the greed of financial institutions, in extreme economic inequalities, in contemporary oppression of the poor, and in structures that oppress and enslave women and children. Lies and deceit that wreak havoc with our public organizations threaten our peace every day. Moreover, we live in a world that practices shared hatred, where small differences are fanned into major problems by unethical leaders, where people are mobilized by common tensions, and where opposing ideologies are encouraged. Our world evidences an inability and worse still an unwillingness to strive for peace. We mourn the loss of a culture of peace.

We need to try always to keep the vision of peace before our minds and our hearts. We know peace is always precarious when there is no respect for human rights, no justice, no ability to live in financial security, and no future worth striving for. But we must maintain an outlook of peace in which all people have rights to truth, freedom, justice, and love. Having had an experience of God's love, we must courageously hold fast to a mindset of peace in spite of threats from all sides. We constantly proclaim the benefits of peace, resolve disagreements without violence or force, and maintain peace in the basic cells of our own life and relationships.

Peace begins with ourselves. Each of us must be at peace; otherwise others will manipulate us into their oppositional, polarizing, hate-filled positions. We advance an agenda of peace not only by identifying disagreements, the causes of the lack of peace, and by removing obstacles to peace, but by creating an environment that prepares for peace. We can get to know our "opponents" better, understanding how they feel about issues and why. Mutual understanding is a first step that breaks artificial justifications for the lack of peace and begins a process of dialogue and mutual appreciation. We can dedicate ourselves to eradicate language and concepts of opposition and establish a language of peace. We can foster common interests in art, history, music, and sport. We can analyze issues together, seeking historical and contemporary insights that can move us forward.

Our efforts to create peace focus on our friends, neighbors, family, church, nation, and the international scene. Peace percolates up from the grassroots. Unless there is ownership at the foundational level, decisions at an international level are not as effective. It is interesting that leading officials in organizations, for example religions or nations, can easily destroy peace and force its destructive influence on others. However, they can almost never reconstruct peace; rather, such rebuilding comes from the base. So, our efforts focus first on friends, neighborhood groups, local churches, cultural sharing, and education of the children. From this level the values of peace percolate up to influence the wider groups. Paralleling these efforts, people at the base can influence major international decisions by pressure on politicians, by making their voices heard, and by only accepting leaders who will work for peace.

Key reflections:

- How do you make a positive difference to other people's lives?
- Are you a loner or do you work best with others?
- Reflect to what extent your talents are at the service of others.
- How much good do you think you do?

Action items:

➢ Examine your life to see what emphasis you give to helping other people.
➢ This coming week, get involved in something in which you have not previously been involved.
➢ Re-establish peace with someone close to you with whom you have lost it.
➢ Promote the talents of someone at work.

Focus questions for one's personal journal.

Focus every day on others
    Do you work well with other people?
    Describe when you were selfish last week.
    Do other people see you as a thoughtful person?
    Do you compare yourself to others? Why?
    What do you think you gain from others?
Bring out the best in others
    Do you make a positive difference to other people's lives?
    How do you bring out the best in others?
    Are you trustworthy?
    Describe how you share—intellectually, organizationally, and personally.
    Describe an episode when you celebrated someone else's success.
    What does sharing your faith mean to you?
Get involved
    Describe why you think some relationships are enriching to you.
    Do you volunteer? Why? Why not?
    How do you make sure your voice is heard by leaders in society and in the church?
    Do you contribute to transforming society?

Plan to do something to improve society.
Work for peace
    Name several examples of a loss of peace.
    Specify some of the benefits of peace.
    Are you at peace with yourself?
    How can you create peace with those around you?

Planning for Strategy Seven: Doing good for others.

1. List three important goals in doing good for others.

2. What are your personal gifts that could help you dedicate your life to doing good for others?

3. Specify any weaknesses that could stunt your doing good for others.

4. What can you do in the short term to achieve these goals?

5. How will you achieve these resolutions?

6. When will you do this?

7. Will you do this alone or with others? With whom?

8. How will you evaluate how successful you have been?

Topics for group discussion or sharing.

1. Let each member of the group make suggestions as to how you can do more good for others.
2. How can the group influence others to be the best they can be?
3. Let the group create an agenda for contributing to the transformation of the local society.
4. Reflect together on what you can do to create peace.

STRATEGY EIGHT
OPEN YOUR MIND AND HEART

Fight against intolerance

We live in a world that is increasingly intolerant, one in which violence, untruthfulness, hate, mutual criticism abound, and people constantly and deliberately do hurtful things to others. Our culture is one of opposition, confrontation, rejection, polarization, and widespread intolerance. People are paid lots of money to be intolerant, and they gather around them a large following of insecure individuals who delight to find their own intolerant attitudes supported by celebrities in politics or religion. These political, social, and religious "leaders" whip their followers into a frenzy over issues that are not central to their original vision, leading to catastrophes like ethnic cleansing, or even to the deliberate, destructive intention of labeling others to demean or destroy them. People develop skills that foster intolerance, challenging people of faith to be equally skilled in opposing it.

Intolerant individuals are generally uninformed or ignorant, either by force of circumstances or by a deliberate closed mindedness—a desire not to learn what other people think or feel. Their deafness to others' views and their unwillingness to search for common ground give rise to a hatred for anyone who thinks differently than themselves. Closed mindedness atrophies thought, but since knowledge is the basis of love it also stunts any ability to grow in understanding and love. Closed mindedness is not a normal characteristic of human beings who innately search for meaning, understanding, and enlightenment. But, people are trained and initiated into closed mindedness generally by social, political, educational, or religious figures. Some local groups or entire nations are known for their open-mindedness, and others for their closed mindedness. However, intolerant behavior is now a serious cultural problem.

Most people do not think they are intolerant. Rather, they have false justification for their behavior. Many think they are being principled, consider their views the only acceptable ones, and see any attempt to understand others as weakness. Our society is riddled with extreme fundamentalism in politics, choice of political parties, judicial practice, approaches to foreign policy, and all sorts of issues in religion. Litmus tests are everywhere, and any divergence from the acceptable, myopic views is rejected, and those who hold different views are despised. Some of the most complicated contemporary issues receive simplistic answers from people who will not or cannot think things through. Such people often act like bulldozers, flattening all other ideas in their path.

People who seek spiritual depth need to reject all forms of intolerant behavior. This will mean first and foremost accepting the need to constantly learn anew, to appreciate that some change and adaptability guarantees the genuineness of values we hold. Never to change means always to live in the past. We must have exceptional listening skills to understand others' words, their deeper yearnings, their struggles, and their hopes. We will need to be people of genuine dialogue, even with others who lack such skills. We can read and study with the desire to be more informed. From time to time we should rethink our own views, either to conclude in reaffirming them or to change them when we notice a loss of focus. So many drag along behind them ideas from the past, emphasize what dedication and discipleship used to be two thousand years ago, and end up worshipping a god from their high school years or a god of their own creation. Intolerant behavior that closes the door on new ways of thinking and doing leads to myopic approaches that quickly destroy society—civic and religious.

Welcome new and different ideas

The call to develop a richer spirituality is essentially the revelation of a new knowledge permeated by love. It is not simply loving more in the same old way, but a conversion that includes a new outlook on life. It is a new way of thinking about one's purpose and end. There is a link between knowledge and love; heart and mind move together in mutual enrichment. Jesus condemned those who had eyes but could not see, ears but could not hear, and said it was because their minds and hearts had grown dull. Unfortunately, we frequently witness an anti-intellectualism in Christianity and in other religions which leads to a worshipping of the past. Rather, we need to accept the importance of knowledge, of ideas that manifest and clarify faith.

Reading, studying, and learning are parts of who we are as faith-filled individuals. Our intellect aids us in clarifying faith and our faith deepens through enriched knowledge. As we read, study, and learn about Scripture, the history of spirituality, Church teachings, and contemporary life, we can welcome new insights into our chosen way of life. It is important that we think, reflect, discern, and discriminate, so that we focus on essentials and not on the trivia that we often see. Part of our journey in life is to purify false images of God expressed in erroneous ideas, and then in a transforming experience we can discover new ways of understanding God.

Part of learning about faith is to welcome ideas that come through re-learning. Like the guardian of the treasure house in Christian Scripture, we seek to value new things and old ones too. Three words catch the stages of the process that people pursue in their constant clarification of faith—root, interpret, and discover. We always refer our ideas concerning faith back to the events of Jesus' life and his teachings and make sure they are rooted in that experience. That, however, is not enough, for it tells us what the challenges of Christianity were two thousand years ago. We also need to come back to the present, interpreting those teachings for today, otherwise they lose relevance. Since change is so rapid today we also need to be ever ready to discover new ways to live our spiritual commitment in contemporary situations, both present and future.

Ideas often become obsolete, and articulations of belief systems become irrelevant as time passes. When people dedicate themselves to beliefs that are irrelevant it is quite sad and disastrous for them personally. Sometimes we need to change formulations of faith, so that what was formerly spirit and life can become equally challenging in new situations, new generations, and new cultures. We need to make conscious decisions to rethink limiting beliefs and find new ways to express our Christian commitment. This is particularly important when the need for change is left unanswered and gradually deteriorates into a crisis of belief. "Crisis" is a word that means "judgment," and it reminds us that when expressions of belief become progressively irrelevant, there arises the need to bring new ideas to the fore and make different judgments regarding how to articulate Christian values in changed circumstances.

Conversion implies being willing to change. When people cling to a known past, we see the fossilization of beliefs and the emergence of arthritic institutions. But, we need the enrichment that comes with a spirit of discovery. Discovery means leaving behind something and searching for something new. It might be a deeper insight, a refinement of our knowledge, a broadening of our understanding, an awareness of a realm of life beyond this one. In study, reflection, and discussion, we can gain new ideas that keep our commitment relevant, vibrant, and meaningful. These are ways we keep our minds open to be filled with a deeper understanding of faith.

Support diversity

Our spiritual commitment impels us to be concerned with everyone's development and calls us to appreciate the mutual enrichment of community. It also reminds us that no life is full without opening and giving of oneself to others whoever they might be. This is the burden of dedication; we must always live and work with others and never take refuge in comfortable isolation. So, we need genuine awareness of other people's views and gifts, knowing that healthy discussion leads to benefits for as many as possible. Faith calls for an appreciation of diversity, and people of faith have something to say on the benefits of diversity. At a time of increased diversity, such people must impact this age of transience with their vision and values.

We have the responsibility to all people to share with them and to receive from them. We cannot condemn others who have different views than our own. Genuine empathy and understanding of differences based on ethnicity, culture, gender, sexual orientation, education, and financial situation, lead to growth in the human community. In fact, each one of us only partially identifies with his or her own community, let alone with others'. We are more diverse than ever; different people have different ways of understanding reality, even within a tradition. Mutual learning between nations, religions, and traditions is always enlightening. This change in consciousness makes us open to insights from others. Honest dialogue can call accepted values into question. At least change calls us to question our own past and to be open to diverse understandings and interpretations.

Part of opening our minds to the richness around us means appreciating differences, maintaining a reconciling approach to others, and wishing others well even before we know them. Differences can sometimes lead to comparisons, subordination, and discrimination. However, sometimes they lead to patriarchy, sexism, control, exaggerated nationalism, lust for political domination, militaristic thinking, intrigues to spread ideologies, labeling of others, and so on. Rather we need strategies to appreciate others. All healthy discussion benefits humankind, and it does not exclude commitment to one's own convictions, nor socially critical approaches to others' views. At the same time, we must be willing to be subjected to the criticism of others. Some people suppose they are thinking for themselves and they are not. Some groups convince themselves they are always right and they are not. We must open our minds and hearts to diverse approaches and values of other human beings, constantly work against polarization, and dedicate ourselves to construct unity.

We not only appreciate differences, we go further and capitalize on diversity. Through serious debate we can see each other's points of view, even using each other's insights to critically correct and change positions. We can help each other by testing our ideas against experience and common sense. Of course we can go further and, sensing we are a global community, we can work for others' personal rights, especially the rights of minorities, and for civic and religious freedoms. Capitalizing on differences and diversity will take lots of patience—"patience" being a word that means "to suffer." However, when we struggle to remove our differences, we find diversity can be our greatest resource.

Be magnanimous

"Magnanimous" is a little-used word today. It refers to someone who has a big soul, or a big spirit, or a big heart. It is a wonderful word to describe a person who longs to deepen his or her spiritual calling. Such a person has freed himself or herself from inherited prejudice and embodies humaneness, sees whatever good there is in others, and feels enriched by other cultures. This kind of person has a refined sense of human community. Such a person opens his or her mind to think well of others, appreciates others' views, and probes others to discover their goodness. Such people are generally vulnerable, being ever ready to allow others to probe their sense of identity as they do to others. They are convinced of the mutual enrichment that comes with opening one's heart to welcome everyone.

People who are magnanimous give themselves generously to others and also gratefully receive from others their self-gift. This new consciousness concerning mutual enrichment begins with awareness of the human and global community and how we grow together. Following this awareness comes a desire for greater understanding of other people, and an opening of one's mind to know someone better. When done honestly, this leads to respect for others' views, whether or not we agree with them. Growth in awareness, understanding, and respect moves a person to acceptance. Even when we find that we cannot accept others' views, we certainly accept them in their own honesty and integrity. In other words we appreciate others more profoundly than ever, and this appreciation challenges us to value other people and their contributions. These components of magnanimity eventually help us to assimilate the goodness of others into a greater consciousness of ourselves as community.

Part of being magnanimous is to examine and redirect our attitudes towards others. First we need to correct mistaken attitudes.

These include very negative but common practices of contemporary society that we witness in our daily news. Vilifying others and their views, categorizing them without knowing them, giving them labels with artificial, assigned meanings, and perpetuating stereotypes and false assumptions. People of faith also carefully identify causes of differences and difficulties, otherwise we too easily think of people as victims and perpetrators. Differences often come with social and economic conditioning. Moreover, we appreciate that differences are not necessarily blocks to healthy communication and mutual appreciation; in fact, they can enhance these dimensions of our lives. Above all, we always presume everyone who is at least moderately mature wants positive relationships.

People who wish to be magnanimous will strategize to become so. This includes resisting all judgmental attitudes towards others—a difficult task in our contemporary society, known for its constant mutual blame. Then, we must learn to excel in listening skills, seeking feedback from others to help us check how we perceive others, and then refocusing. These people also cultivate a new self-awareness that includes others as integral to a vision of themselves. There is no way to avoid taking risks in deepening relationships with others. In fact, risk taking is integral to the strategy of a magnanimous person. Finally, the goal of each of these strategies is always the same—to let others find a place in our hearts, even those with whom we disagree. Being magnanimous contributes so positively to opening our minds to be enriched by new ideas.

At the same time we are not naïve nor are we fools. There is an increasing number of individuals and groups who are totally given to intolerance. They earn money—lots of it, and gain supporters exclusively because they are obsessed with bigotry and intolerance. Without mutuality and openness there can be no genuine dialogue. Spiritually dedicated individuals must struggle when results are possible but should not waste time.

Enrich our view of life

If we fight against intolerance, welcome new ideas, support diversity, and deal with other people with magnanimity, we will clearly enrich our own lives. None of these commitments will water down our own convictions; rather they will give our convictions a more solid and a broader foundation. Opening our minds in these and other ways is a wonderful dimension of the commitment to spiritual growth.

Several of the strategies of spiritual growth that we have considered imply a greater appreciation of the fact that we are part of a community of people who share common values. Each of us is incomplete in himself or herself but part of a greater whole. Scripture says we are all separate members of one body. We need each other and are incomplete without others. Moreover, being parts of a greater whole tones down the negative effects of individualism and isolationism. So, we live as a community, appreciating our interdependence. We become who we are called to be through mutual respect and mutual enrichment. This leads us to shared vision, collaboration with others, and an awareness of the values of fusion and synergy.

We keep our minds open to ideas and insights into faith because of our conviction that God is present to everyone, deep within their spirit, calling them to transformation. So, opening our mind is not only an intellectual exercise but part of our spirituality. We encounter the call of God not only deep within our own hearts but also through others, even those from different belief systems or religions. Perhaps only with and through others can we discover what it is we lack.

People who seek spiritual growth open their minds in pursuit of wisdom; they study, reflect, share, and meditate on truths that enrich life. However, wisdom is more than truths arrived at through knowledge. It is an insight into faith or an interpretation of faith that also results from reflection on experiences—one's own and others'. Such people are reflective, open to inspiration from whatever source, and appreciative of a sense of mystery and awe that comes from learning from the dedication of others. Such people must always be enthusiastic learners, seeking whatever helps them know and love the God of their faith.

Key reflections:

- What are your own biases in dealing with people?
- Are you tolerant or intolerant towards others?

- Are the key components of your faith rooted in Jesus' life and experience?
- Re-examine your own attitudes to diversity.
- Consider whether others view you as open minded or narrow minded.

Action items:

➤ Make an effort this week to enrich your knowledge of your faith.
➤ Do something positive with someone who thinks differently than you do.
➤ Examine your faith to see how its expression has changed over the years.
➤ Consciously learn something good from someone else this week.

Focus questions for one's personal journal.

Fight against intolerance

Have you become more or less tolerant in recent years?

Name an individual or group to whom you are closed-minded.

Is there an issue about which you think you are principled and others think you are intolerant?

Describe a situation where you learned something from someone you dislike or oppose.

Welcome ideas

What place does learning play in your life?

Do you read and study about faith?

Do you excel or fail in rooting, interpreting, and discovering faith?

How has your understanding of your Christian commitment changed since high school?

What is new about your understanding of your faith?

Support diversity

How do you appreciate diversity?

Are you willing to change?

Describe what you like about someone who is very different than you.

Why do you think diversity is a positive value for community?

Be magnanimous

Would other people describe you as "big hearted"?

Do you honestly respect others' views?

Do you ever "put down" someone else?

Describe your listening skills.

Enrich your view of life

How can others help you to be a more "complete" human being?

Describe a situation where you experienced God's call through someone else.

Are you a lifelong learner?

Planning for Strategy Eight: Opening your mind.

1. List three important goals in opening your mind.

2. What are your personal gifts that could help you attain these goals?

3. Specify any weaknesses that could stunt the opening of your mind.

4. What can you do in the short term to achieve these goals?

5. How will you achieve these resolutions?

6. When will you do this?

7. Will you do this alone or with others? With whom?

8. How will you evaluate how successful you have been?

Topics for group discussion or sharing.

1. Let the group establish a plan to fight intolerance in the local community.
2. Each member can describe a new idea that has enriched his or her life.
3. How can this group find ways of supporting diversity?
4. Can the group find ways of being open-minded while preserving principles?

STRATEGY NINE
STAY THE COURSE

Persevere with determination

As people searching for depth in our spiritual commitment, we need to persevere in our dedication to each of these ten strategies. None can be episodic or sporadic. Rather, they all need to be permanent facets of our living commitment. There is no faith without perseverance. Moreover, our contemporary society's values operate against faithfulness, for they focus on this world and immediate satisfaction and have little thought for a realm of life beyond this one. However, we want to be firm in our fidelity, dedicated with determination—a word that means bringing our commitment to its anticipated end. We have seen that faith is always linked to hope; it is hope that challenges us to persevere with determination, never abandoning the chosen path of faith.

The life of spiritual growth is not for the fainthearted. Those who choose to persevere will need courage or fortitude. This vital quality shows itself in two ways: one positive and the other negative—or at least initially it seems negative. Fortitude includes holding fast to what is good and having the strength to attack what is contrary to the goodness of our values. However, fortitude also includes facing serious challenges, enduring hardships, and even accepting the suffering that comes with faithfully living the consequences of dedication. While some consider this second dimension to be negative or passive, people like Gandhi or Martin Luther King have shown how powerful and positive non-violent resistance can be. Christian fortitude also includes patience and calmness; otherwise it can deteriorate into frustration, anger, and resentment on the one hand, or fear and weakness on the other.

The fortitude needed to persevere with determination in our dedication to the values of faith is one of four cardinal virtues in Christianity. So called because they are four key qualities that open the door to a life of integral Christian commitment (cardinal=hinge). These four qualities are fortitude, justice, prudence, and temperance, and they are closely related to each other. To live genuine fortitude, we must first be prudent; otherwise our determination can carry us to all kinds of exaggerations. Then, in living with determination, we need to maintain a sense of justice; otherwise we can with false zeal impose our views on others, thinking we are always right. Then, we live our fortitude with temperance, maintaining a sense of balance in what we do and how we treat others. These four qualities are most effective when linked to the three theological virtues of faith, hope, and charity.

Persevering with determination is a form of integrity. It means honestly living the consequences of our vision of life, so that what we do outwardly manifests what we think inwardly. Our inner and outer realities are the same. Fortitude and integrity are two qualities that complement each other. Integrity means speaking and living the truth with courage but also accepting one's own shortcomings and failures. As people of integrity, we know what motivates us; we know what we stand for and what we do not stand for. Only then can we faithfully respond with inner mastery.

We call "martyrs" those early Christians who persevered in their faith in spite of suffering. "Martyr" is a word which means giving testimony. Nowadays, we too want to stay the course and bear witness to our faith with determination. It will unquestionably imply enduring suffering for the good causes of faith. The obstacles and hardships are different today, but they are equally real. Opposition can come from people who have a different world view, obstacles arise from individuals who have exclusively social, sexual agendas but use religious language to express themselves, and others impose their myopic views of belief as tests of genuine dedication. Hardships also come from well meaning but theologically unqualified religious leaders who equate their own views with faith. We also acknowledge increasing numbers of insecure individuals who establish a culture of fear in which people of faith are continually criticized. We need to dedicate ourselves to living the faith and doing the good that results from faith, and doing all this with integrity and persevering fortitude.

Maintain faith

We strive to maintain the quality of our dedication through all the ups and downs of life. We endeavor to live differently because of the experience that gave rise to our life of dedication, to be always firm in acknowledging the faith that motivates us. Moreover, while the original experience of God's intervention in our lives will never change, our understanding and appreciation of it will mature as we gain new insights into the experience. Living our faith is a journey along a straight and narrow path that is steep as it ascends to the call of God. The upward climb is not regular but has valleys and peaks. Furthermore, what we think is the final peak in our ascent is often nothing more than an intermediate goal before journeying through other valleys and peaks that still lie ahead. These valleys are crises that we must confront, work through, and then we can climb again. How we handle the crises that we encounter in striving to be faithful leads to maturity in faith. Our dedication grows and matures through crises, and God allows these crises so that we will find new ways of knowing and loving God. Spiritual writers and mystics call these crises "dark nights," and no matter how painful these experiences are—and they will be, we must stay the course and let God draw us forward to a deeper understanding of what our lives should be like.

When we journey in our spiritual life we cannot see what lies ahead, and that may be for the best. We discover that God is not like what we thought God would be, and then we also find that God does not act towards us in the ways we thought God would. This double experience helps us to change the way we think of God—moving away from childish images and letting God be who God wishes to be for us. At the same time, staying the course and maintaining faith also brings us face to face with God's personal relationship with us. When we yearn for God to be close to us, God often withdraws. When, because of our failures, we would wish God were afar off, God instead comes close by. Sometimes when we expect God to be distant from us we catch glimpses of a supportive presence. We learn God's love of us is a dark experience, a guiding experience, and a transforming experience. The original experience that gave rise to faith is the start of a journey to greater maturity in understanding God.

Many people we meet, including some good friends who have given a lot of thought to matters of faith, belief, and religion, inform us that they are atheists or agnostics. Many others who have given little thought to these serious issues act as if they have no significant beliefs. Some do not hesitate to indicate their surprise that we are people of faith. They give the impression they think we are naïve, lacking in perceptive intelligence, and still think we will eventually grow out of it. They challenge us explicitly or implicitly. Nowadays, going to Church or to another religious institution seems more acceptable than insisting we have profound faith. Church-going is socially acceptable, faith is difficult to grasp. But, we must maintain faith with enthusiasm and relentless dedication. Moreover, we must be ready to go public with our vision of this world, our experience of God, and our sense of personal destiny—and we must stay the course.

Accept insecurity and ambiguity

Our journey to spiritual maturity does not start with us but with God who is the end of the journey. We are not laboriously striving to reach our goal, but rather being drawn by God to the goal of life. We are not giving but receiving—faith is not some knowledge we earn but a gift for which we are unworthy. Our task in the journey is not to achieve the goal ourselves but to let go of false values that hold us back. Those aspects of our awareness that we think we are sure of are precisely what we must leave behind. The journey is away from former images of God, religion, self, others, and the roles each has in our lives, as we are drawn towards new understandings of God, religion, self, others, and the impact they can have on our lives. This is not an experience of certainty in our knowledge of God, but the insecurity of discovering that what we did know is no use anymore. We must leave it aside and open ourselves to be enlightened in a new way and to discover a greater dimension of truth.

We can persevere with confidence in our journey of faith, knowing God is drawing us forward. But, we will need to balance the confidence with humility. Arrogantly clinging to what we knew will destroy our opportunity to encounter God. Rather, having experienced God's love, we are down to earth or humble (humus=ground or earth). In other words, we are aware of our limitations and also of our nothingness before God. Humility not only modifies our attitudes towards God during the journey of faith, but also our attitudes towards others, calling us to accept their human weaknesses and hopes, as we do our own. So, humility naturally leads to love and gratitude to God, and compassionate care of others. Humility allows us to honestly develop our relationship to God and to others, and it is an essential characteristic of those who accept insecurity and courageously stay the course in their journey of faith.

We are convinced that we have glimpsed another horizon of life beyond this one. It is not a crystal clear experience that gives certitude but one that gives sufficient hope to change the way we think and live. Generally, such people have questions about their choices and also appreciate how others can arrive at conclusions that are different than their own. There is an unhealthy tendency in religions to offer their followers certainty when there is no certainty. They claim certitude on issues both theological and moral that cannot be proved. If everything was clear beyond question, everyone could be persuaded to follow. Even great spiritual leaders have doubts of faith, as we read in their biographies and spiritual writings. In our journey of faith a little skepticism is always in order, and we also need to welcome and celebrate the gift of doubt. Faith is a risk; we need courage to make the choice and accept the insecurity it brings.

Staying the course on the journey of faith can be a lonely experience. We need to be content with ourselves, enjoy the solitude, and find satisfaction in silence, emptiness, and stillness. Part of the journey is the self-emptying that precedes the opportunities for fulfillment. We empty ourselves of former ways of knowing and loving God and others, and only then can we be filled with a new understanding and love. We also need to sense our own emptiness, even savor it, so that we truly realize that we are in need of help, guidance, and transformation. Our quest is basically the process of surrender, as we give ourselves to God's transforming action in our hearts. This surrender is the single-minded choice to do what is asked of us. It is the painful uprooting of former vision and values and the willingness to say "yes" to this new journey, leaving behind what we cherished and walking courageously to the unknown.

Risk all

Writers and spiritual leaders in every generation describe the journey of faith as the climbing of a mountain. Certainly there are parallels. You need training, the climb is arduous, you cannot afford to keep stopping on the journey, and you feel lonely but should always have others in your company. If you stop on the way and either go no further or even turn back, you deprive yourself of one of the great experiences of your life. People who climb will tell you there is no experience like being at the top of the mountain. The higher you climb the more awesome the scenery. When you reach the top, everything looks different—the scenery, the world, and yourself. There is likewise wonderful excitement in journeying in faith—it is a great quest, a hero's journey, a transforming experience. No one can understand how a climber can endure so much in training and the pains and struggles of the ascent, unless he or she has also been to the top—then it is easy to understand.

The journey of faith is not a journey of knowledge. It is more a journey of unknowing rather than knowing. It is arduous and painful, but what motivates us is love. In fact, it is a quest for a deeper relationship of love with God that overflows to others too. We seek God through hardships and darkness to experience greater union and renewal. Basically, the journey is one of making decisions in light of love. For this we are willing to risk everything. This journey is like a personal exodus away from a vision and values that enslaved us, to a vision and values that liberate us.

Staying the course is difficult, and as we have seen it can be lonely, but many find encouragement in a variety of support systems. One's spouse or family can help when they share similar values. Friends can be important, especially those with whom we have shared the struggles and joys of our search in faith. A mentor or advisor will undoubtedly bring honest assessment of our efforts, be a sounding board for our ideas, always speak the truth, and give advice that challenges us. We should surround ourselves with wise people who can inspire, motivate, question, and guide. At the same time, we need to read, study, and reflect on issues relating to our journey. The biographies of other faith-filled individuals can also enrich our understanding, indicating that problems we face are not unique, and illuminating solutions to common struggles.

This life journey is a risk, for it is a discovery of a previously unknown world. It is a quest that is filled with risks. We persevere with determination, maintain faith, accept insecurity, and courageously stay the course. The journey is filled with risks, but there comes a point when the only risk is not continuing; we cannot do anything else except take the risk. The enthusiasm for what lies ahead motivates us, and the only real choice we have is to continue. We need to continue to proclaim our faith. This will include challenging wrongdoing against the values of faith. Then, we must not be silent but rather never let rejection of faith go unanswered. Above all, we must stay the course with fortitude, maintain the quality of faith, accept the impossibility of security, and risk all for the goal that lies ahead.

Key reflections:
- Reflect on whether you are fainthearted in your commitment or whether you live it with fortitude.
- Is your fortitude in faith perfected with prudence, justice, and temperance?
- Consider whether your outer self truly reflects your inner values.
- What are the key obstacles and hardships you encounter in living your faith?

Action items:
- Examine your daily life to see how you maintain your daily commitment in spite of the challenges of contemporary society.
- Give some time this week to considering how your image of God has changed since your formative years.
- List three reasons to show why you think you are actively journeying in faith.
- Read a biography of a great figure known for the quality of his or her faith-filled commitment.

Focus questions for one's personal journal.

Persevere with determination

> Are you a person who perseveres in faith?
>
> What does "fortitude" mean to you?
>
> How do you show fortitude, justice, prudence, and temperance in daily life?
>
> What do you stand for?
>
> Describe how you bear witness to your faith with determination.

Maintain faith

> Give examples of how your faith has matured.
>
> Where are you on the journey of life?
>
> Are you surprised at how God acts towards you? Why? Why not?
>
> Are you enthusiastic about your faith?

Accept insecurity

> Give an example of something that you accepted with conviction but no longer do.
>
> What does humility mean to you?
>
> Describe doubts that have come into your life.
>
> Do you ever feel empty? Is this good or bad?

Risk all

> Is there a mountain you want to climb in your spiritual life?
>
> Give some recent examples of when you made decisions in light of love.
>
> What are your support systems for your faith?
>
> What is the risk of faith for you?

Planning for Strategy Nine: Staying the course.

1. List three important goals that would help you to stay the course.

2. What are your personal gifts that could help you attain these goals?

3. Specify any weaknesses that could stunt your growth in this area.

4. What can you do in the short term to achieve these goals?

5. How will you achieve these resolutions?

6. When will you do this?

7. Will you do this alone or with others? With whom?

8. How will you evaluate how successful you have been?

Topics for group discussion or sharing.
1. Let the group discuss the meaning of perseverance.
2. How has faith matured for each one in the group?
3. Why do members feel insecure in their spiritual journey?
4. Discuss the risks of faith.

STRATEGY TEN
LIVE YOUR LIFE TO THE FULL

Strive for a greater share in existence

The spiritual challenge that comes with faith impels us to strive for a greater share in existence. Faith gives us insight into the meaning of life, a sense of community belonging, an understanding of right and wrong, and a sense of wonder and awe. In fact, with dedication we live at the level of mystery, and feel called to develop every facet of our lives in order to become our authentic selves. The various strategies we have considered come together in the kind of lives we live and help us achieve our potential. This is our spirituality, and it refers to becoming a person in the fullest sense, animated and motivated by the values of faith, and enriched by sharing within the faith community. This response includes all aspects of life in depth and in extent.

The life that results from a dedication to the strategies we have seen implies in each of us an awareness of a call to continual growth in life, both personally and as community. We feel we cannot stand still but need to be dedicated to something or someone bigger than ourselves, and this clarifies for us our own place in this world and our own destiny. It is the challenge to make every effort to be the best of which we are capable. At the same time, we seek to be critical of our own lives and values, having the humility to leave aside the worst of ourselves, and having the courage to develop our best selves. Fidelity to this response gives meaning to our lives.

Our spiritual commitment has four important focuses. First, we emphasize both individual and communal growth at the same time. We strive to become mature individuals and mature members of community. The former enriches the latter and then overflows in contribution to the wider communities—civic, national, and international. The second focus is to be an influential presence in the events of our world. The values that motivate us in spiritual dedication can have a transforming effect on world events, family life, social and political action, and ecological concerns; our life must have a purpose and impact real issues. The third focus of our lives is a commitment to the service of others. This is part of the movement away from self-centeredness to focus on others. The fourth focus of life is that our spiritual commitment is liberational; it emphasizes the need to free oneself and others from all forms of oppression, slavery, and injustice. So, it becomes redemptive from the sins of this world and open to freedom.

The way of life that results from spiritual commitment is our way of becoming who we are meant to be. More than anything else, it is the conscious effort to integrate all aspects of life on the basis of our spiritual experience of ultimate values. So, we must integrate life, making sure our convictions and their resulting lifestyle touch every area of human experience. The life of continual spiritual growth is without doubt the finest way in which each of us can attain our human potential. It is not departmentalized from other aspects of life; it is the only way to give full value and meaning to the human effort to strive for a greater share in existence.

Affirm values and vision

The life of the spirit to which we give ourselves has several characteristics. It is a transitory manifestation of perennial values. The motivating values of life are rooted in the core values of our original experience of God's love. However, as circumstances change, we will need to live out these values in new ways. These values evolve, and we need to be open to more relevant ways of living these core values, as we move from one situation to another.

Our spiritual commitment permeates every aspect of life. It starts with actual daily experiences of each of us with our own history, but it challenges us to relate differently to self, others, and the world because of the personal spiritual experience that calls us to transformation. Part of this commitment is self-acceptance, rejoicing in oneself, and celebrating one's gifts. So, self-knowledge, peace, joy, and enthusiasm, all become part of allowing this dedication to permeate our entire lives.

This life that results from spiritual dedication is a form of creative self-fulfillment. It includes a healthy acceptance of our embodied lives, for we express our inner feelings through our bodies. This life does not emphasize only inner, spiritual, supernatural elements of life, as if they were better than outer, natural, and material components of life. Rather, it optimistically stresses the directing of the whole of life to God. We must become our true selves, capitalizing on every aspect of our personalities. This commitment has no interest in escapism into pre-packaged and recycled spirituality of times past.

This life includes a sense of humility, the humble awareness that we need to struggle daily to respond to the call of faith. We are always ready to learn from others, to be always attentive listeners to our world, and to be ever open to search for truth. Humility will make us compassionate to those who suffer, sensitive to any discrimination of others, and always willing to dialogue and learn. Humility is important, above all because we are aware that growth in life is God's work and not ours.

Our life of commitment develops with others and not in some solitary experience. Spiritually dedicated individuals share life, give themselves in service, cooperate with others, and collaborate in shared enterprises. We must let go of all forms of selfishness and constantly and confidently grow with others in community. This includes commitment to grow within institutions that at times can be awkward and at times gracious. We cannot neglect the need to work within institutions—civic and religious—for in contributing to their transformation, they can better the world.

Daily life includes a positive approach to creation, whether statically in the world around us or dynamically in the historical and contemporary achievements of humanity. People enjoy and appreciate the environment around them, seeing it as a guru that teaches with its own rhythms and balances. In understanding the world and its development a person finds confirmation of the abundant love of God. A sympathetic understanding of the world must also include one's own physical life, health, changes, and hardships, and the challenges to healthy living and self-care.

This life is especially characterized by a life of reflection and prayer. The original experience of God's mercy, forgiveness, compassion, and love challenges each person to be a person of interiority and reflection, what we might even call an everyday mystic. Thrilled by the profound spiritual experience, an individual longs to return to re-experience the encounter with God. All other characteristics prepare us for this one. What we share with others is the fruit of our experience of the living God. It is this experience that impels us to participate in spreading the love of God in our world.

Commit to what is real and true

We are people transformed by our encounter with God, and we strive to daily assimilate the values of this experience. The most immediate consequence is our conviction that there is more in life than meets the eye; there is a world that is not immediately apparent. Our experience teaches us that there are two horizons to life, and they are intimately linked. We discover in ourselves a zone that naturally yearns for transcendent reality, and we live at this level of mystery, where we are enthralled by enduring truths. Everything we think and do is transformed by this awareness of a relationship between our everyday life and a realm of life that gives meaning to this one.

People dedicated to spiritual growth should naturally identify with the transcendent. Deep within each of us there is a yearning for union with God. This process of discovering the potential for growth that lies within us includes distancing ourselves from the accumulation of religious devotions and entering with simplicity into our own hearts. No one paints a great cathedral, one sandblasts it. Likewise, we seek the richness of life not by adding on more religious practices but by touching ultimate goodness and love that lie within us. Encountering the everlasting call of God in our own hearts, we then see that our experience guides the course of life. We need to pay attention to the connections between our own yearnings for fulfillment and the call of another realm of life, for we live here in this world while always being elsewhere too.

Whatever our level of dedication, we have glimpsed the reality of God's love for us. It may have been merely a glimpse, but it is one of the most real experiences of life. What other people say of our experience—it is subjective, it is a sublimation of other needs, it is the result of family or cultural ties—means nothing to us. Certainly, as we have seen, we may often question our own faith; share a little healthy doubt or skepticism, but more than anything we know we encountered a mystery that impacts every facet of our lives.

Throughout these reflections on ten strategies of spiritual growth we have consistently seen that belief systems and religions can at times be very helpful and supportive. They synthesize human understandings of God, offer ways to goodness, clarify common obstacles, and suggest helpful virtues. As people who have had a profound experience that became the object of faith, we know that we learn less of God through instruction and accumulated information (the way of knowing) than we do through the experiences that shatter previous knowledge (the way of unknowing). Such a person experiences God's love, justice, mercy, call, and challenge in the depths of his or her heart and accepts all vitally and not merely intellectually. These encounters are real.

While appreciating two horizons of life, we gradually integrate both into one total way of life. Spiritual writers speak about living in the presence of God, or enjoying the fullness of the present moment. Certainly, when we truly integrate the experience into life, it enables us to live in both horizons at the same time. We live here having already been elsewhere. I have always felt called to be here and elsewhere at the same time. For me, living here is always different because of efforts to be elsewhere. Having experienced God's love, we commit ourselves to what is real and true.

Make faith real

The life that results from faith matures in expression as we ourselves mature. This life will be different in early years than in retirement years; different for less educated than for more educated; different for women than for men, and so on. All will seek to manifest in their own originality the experience that transformed their lives. But, new emphases will emerge for all of us. Daily prayers will no longer be as important as fostering a reflective life. Occasional good deeds will no longer be as important as a life of goodness for others. Self-denial and self-sacrifice will no longer be as important as being a person for others. Rituals will not be as important as the ecstasy of profound experience. Accumulating more will be insignificant alongside the building of a life of hope.

At the same time, people of spiritual growth will emphasize simplicity and intensity of the present moment and always remember the experience that transformed their lives. They will stress authentic, unconditional love of self, others, the world, and God. Each day they will strive to transcend themselves and become other-centered and give themselves to the common good of people everywhere. Then, they will accept the fact that they have a mission and a destiny in this world; personally called by God to help others live life to the full.

We make our lives real by a conscious personal commitment. Nowadays, faith is a matter of personal choice not an inherited tradition. We are not passive but active in appreciating the importance of responsible dedication. For Christians, this would imply a rediscovery of their baptismal vocation, and for others a rediscovery of the initial great call they felt in the moment of faith.

Living faith does not refer primarily to the effort we contribute, but rather to what God is doing in us. So, a hallmark of our life of faith is awareness that life is grace and gift of God. Our contribution is to be open, receptive, and aware of our emptiness without God.

Nowadays, our faith calls us to take responsibility for moral choices. As circumstances change our conscience evaluates differently. We facilitate good decisions by self-evaluation, prayer, prudence, knowledge of faith, and consensus of other people of faith.

We cannot prove our dedication in our spare time, but only in the major moments of each day. This includes the importance of a right approach to our working life. Our fidelity to the values of spiritual life is severely tested during working hours when we are generally alone. How we deal with work—with honesty, generosity, service, and quality, proves our commitment.

The life that results from faith includes a readiness to work for community at all levels—family, friends, church, political, and international life. Our struggle-filled efforts to build community can bring transformation to every level of life.

An important contemporary aspect of life is joy—enjoying the good things of life. This, too, must become part of a life of faith.

We are the only generation in human history that has two lives, a working life and a leisure life, and we also need to permeate the latter with the values of faith.

We have already considered the importance of reflection and prayer, participation in local religious institutions' life and worship, our outreach in service to others, and a call to challenge the injustices of our world. We will need to develop all these aspects of life that result from faith, so we are always making our faith real.

The life that results from a spiritual transformation is our way of becoming who we are capable of being; it is a striving for a greater existence. This life is our way of affirming the values and vision of spiritual life. Above all, it becomes a way of integrating this present horizon of life with the realm of life beyond this one. While being drawn to transcendent life we keep our feet on the ground, and we dedicate ourselves to assuring that our spiritual dedication is made real in the practicalities of daily life.

As people of faith we look back to the spiritual experience that transformed our lives and do so with excitement and enthusiasm. We are called to fullness of life, and must never stand still if we wish to get there. These strategies are deliberate action items that help us implement the vision to which we feel called.

Key reflections:
- Think about what you learned from being close to God in your own experience of faith.
- Think about how you experience the fullness of life.
- Consider how you can become a more reflective person.
- Does your knowledge of being elsewhere affect how you live in the here and now?

Action items:
- Examine your life according to the four key focuses: individual and communal growth, transforming presence to the world, commitment to service, and liberational.
- Make concrete decisions to implement your own sense of mission in the plan of God.

> ➢ Review the quality of your working life to assure it is influenced by your faith.
> ➢ Spend time refocusing your commitment and identify new ways of showing it.

Focus questions for one's personal journal.

Strive for a greater share in existence

How does faith help you reach your full potential?

What are you dedicated to that is bigger than yourself?

How are you less self-centered than you used to be?

What would you lose if you were not a faith-filled person?

Affirm values and vision

How has faith evolved for you?

How has your faith led you to relate differently to other people?

Does faith impact every aspect of your daily life? If it does— how? If not—why not?

How do you see God active in your life?

How has your relating to institutions been affected by your faith?

What have you learned from the rhythms of the world?

Do you nurture your faith in prayer?

Commit to what is real and true

Comment on the idea that there is more to life than meets the eye.

How do you live in this world while at times being elsewhere?

Describe a recent experience of God's love for you.

What does "the way of unknowing" mean to you?

How do you experience the presence of God?

Describe some changes in your expression of religion.

What is your mission and destiny in this world?

Describe how daily life is influenced by your dedication to faith.

Planning for Strategy Ten: Living life to the full.

1. List three important goals you can set yourself to live life to the full.

2. What are your personal gifts that could help you attain these goals?

3. Specify any weaknesses that could stunt your growth in these efforts.

4. What can you do in the short term to achieve these goals?

5. How will you achieve these resolutions?

6. When will you do this?

7. Will you do this alone or with others? With whom?

8. How will you evaluate how successful you have been?

Topics for group discussion or sharing.

1. How is the group's life richer because of the members' faith?
2. What is the group's vision for itself?
3. Let each member share an experience of when he or she caught a glimpse of a realm of life beyond this one.
4. Share suggestions on how to make faith more real in daily life.

CONTEMPORARY SPIRITUALITY FOR CHRISTIAN ADULTS

Embrace the new enthusiasm in the Church and nurture your Christian commitment with just ten minutes of reflection a week.

A new spirit is stirring in the Church. We must overcome the failures of the past and prepare ourselves for a future of growth and responsibility. Let us rekindle spiritual insight, accept our spiritual destiny, and refocus on the essential teaching of salvation. While many have left the institutional churches, and sadly may never return, perhaps the challenge to renewal of Pope Francis may re-attract them to the essentials of Christian commitment. The Church will grow and benefit from an informed laity who deepens knowledge of the essential teachings of faith. I created a book with short sections, targeting areas of personal reflection valuable for individuals and discussion groups for this purpose.

Rediscovering Jesus' Priorities.

This book urges readers to look again at Jesus' teachings and identify the major priorities. It is a call to rethink the essential components of a living and vital Christianity and a challenge to rediscover the basic values Jesus proclaimed. Use the book for a short meditation and personal examination, as a self-guided retreat to call yourself to renewed dedication to Jesus' call, or for group discussion and renewed application of Jesus' teachings.

All books available at Amazon.com

Spirituality and leadership blog
leonarddoohan.wordpress.com

Spirituality and John of the Cross blog
johnofthecrosstoday.wordpress.com

More about all my books
leonarddoohan.com

Made in the USA
San Bernardino, CA
13 July 2018